LETTERS TO THE HON'BLE PRIME MINISTER

PART IX

(THE BOOK IS A THINK TANK, COMPRISING INNOVATIVE AND ORIGINAL CONCEPTS BY THE AUTHOR, AN ORIGINAL THINKER, OFFERING SUGGESTIONS FOR MAKING BHARAT A DEVELOPED COUNTRY AND ACHIEVING GLOBAL PEACE)

Dr. Nanda Nandan Das

NOTION PRESS

NOTION PRESS

India. Singapore. Malaysia.

Author:

Dr. Nanda Nandan Das, Original Thinker
D.Sc, D.Litt, PDF (South Korea), PhD
(Road),PhD(Building), M.S.W, B.Sc. (Engg), LLB,
F.I.E, M.I.R.C, M.I.B.C
Former Secretary, Works, Government of Odisha
Former Chairman, O.B & C.C
Chairman, People's Welfare Suggestion Forum
Ex-Chairman, Odisha Durneeti Sangharsa Mancha
Ex-Team Leader, Mott. Mac Donald
Ex-Consultant, POSCO-INDIA
Ex-State Quality Monitor (SQM), Odisha
Address: Plot. No. 2024, Chintamaniswar Area, Bhubaneswar-751006,
Odisha, India
Mob. +91-9437617604
E-mail: nandanandan_das@yahoo.com
COUNTRIES VISITED- USA, CANADA, BRITAIN, GERMANY, FRANCE, SWITZERLAND, LIECHTENSTEIN, NETHERLAND, BELGIUM, ITALY, AUSTRIA, VATICAN, DUBAI, ABU DHABI, SOUTH AFRICA, AUSTRALIA, NEW ZEALAND, FIJI, CHINA, JAPAN, THAILAND, MALAYSIA, SINGAPORE, NEPAL AND SRI LANKA.

Editor:
Er. Shree Nandan Das

Chief Editor:
Prof. Purnima Mitra
First Edition: 2024

Dedicated to
    Entire Global Family to live in peace in
                    Esteemed Mother Earth

CONTENTS

THE AUTHOR'S VIEW

The contents of this book are a compilation of my suggestions to the Hon'ble Prime Minister of India, focusing on various strategies for the nation's development. I firmly believe that all humanity is one family, united under the care of Mother Earth, irrespective of nationality or identity. As inhabitants of this shared planet, it is our collective duty to strive for harmony and well-being. My contributions to the United Nations reflect my unwavering commitment to achieving global peace.

Every concept presented in this book is original, born from spontaneous moments of inspiration, often at the most unusual hours. These ideas were later developed into articles and, following rigorous discussions with experts, were shared with the Hon'ble Prime Minister and other relevant authorities. My work is also documented in twelve volumes titled Letters to the Hon'ble Prime Minister, which are available online. These volumes address critical challenges facing the country and propose pathways to global harmony. I am confident that if any developing or underdeveloped nation adopts these principles with sincerity, they will experience significant progress.

One of the defining moments in my journey was the warm reception I received from the Hon'ble Prime Minister of Bharat, Shri Narendra Modi

Ji, in 2019. It fills me with immense satisfaction to see many of my ideas reflected in his speeches at the United Nations and in the Indian Parliament.

प्रधान मंत्री
Prime Minister

New Delhi
आश्विन 12, शक संवत् 1946
04 October, 2024

Shri Nanda Nandan Das Ji,

Heartfelt gratitude to you for sending warm birthday wishes. I am overwhelmed to receive greetings from my family members such as yourself from across the country.

Your trust, support and cooperation are my real treasure. Your affectionate words fill me with new energy to strive in service of the nation. In the third term of our government, my resolve to fulfil the aspirations of the people and take India to great heights of progress has further strengthened.

Powered by the ability of our people and the skills of our youth, we have been setting new benchmarks in development over the last 10 years. *Amrit Kaal* is an opportunity to scale up our efforts to build a developed, inclusive and self-reliant nation.

The contribution of every Indian towards the progress of the nation is deeply valued.

With best wishes for your good health, happiness and prosperity.

Yours,

(Narendra Modi)

Shri Nanda Nandan Das
Plot- 2024, Chintamaniswar Area
Bhubaneswar, District- Khordha
Odisha- 751006

One cherished memory is a letter I received from the Hon'ble Prime Minister dated October 4, 2024. It stands as a source of immense pride not only for me but also for my family and community. The Hon'ble Prime Minister's words, "Your trust, support, and cooperation are my real treasure. Your affectionate words fill me with new energy to strive in service of the nation. In the third term of our government, my resolve to fulfil the aspirations of the people and take India to great heights of progress has further strengthened," left me overwhelmed and deeply moved. I feel profound gratitude for such an encouraging acknowledgment. I hope my work continues to inspire progress, unity, and peace for all.

Beyond these contributions, I have also made discoveries related to fundamental aspects of Earth sciences, including the Earth's rotation on its axis in an anti-clockwise direction (resulting in day and night), the Moon's revolution around the Earth over a month, and the existence of the Earth's magnetic field. These findings were communicated to ISRO and the Hon'ble Prime Minister as evidence of my dedication to advancing knowledge.

Dr. Nanda Nandan Das, Original Thinker,
The Author

EDITORIAL DESK

Dr. Nanda Nandan Das, born on December 21, 1943, in the village of Baudpur, Bhadrak, Odisha, Bharat, is a distinguished figure in the realm of engineering and administrative services. He embarked on his professional journey after obtaining a B.Sc. (Engg.) from UCE, Burla, in 1965. His illustrious career culminated when he retired as the Secretary of Works Govt. of Odisha and Chairman of O.B & C.C on December 31, 2001. His unwavering dedication to duty and innovative problem-solving abilities made him a trailblazer, consistently demonstrating that nothing is insurmountable.

Recognition and accolades have followed Dr. Nanda Nandan Das throughout his career:

State Awards: Six prestigious honours from "The Institution of Engineers India, Odisha Centre, Bhubaneswar" in 2002, 2003, 2004, 2006, 2016, and 2017.

National Recognition: Rashtriya Gourav Award - Certificate of Excellence presented by Dr. G.V.G. Krishnamurty, the Honourable Former Election Commissioner, in 2004.

International Acknowledgment: PDF, South Korea, recognized Dr. Nanda Nandan Das's contributions in 2016.

- Gopabandhu Das Samman in 2019
- Madhusudan Das Samman in 2020.
- Original Thinker Award in 2018.
- Lifetime Achievement Award from 'The Institution of Engineers India, Odisha Centre' in 2013.
- Felicitation by ISTE, Odisha Section, in 2017.

Dr. Nanda Nandan Das's remarkable achievements extend beyond his professional life. He has saved four lives from perilous situations in rivers like the Ganges, Salandi, and Indirabati. His globetrotting experiences have taken him to numerous countries, including Britain, Paris, Germany, Italy, Switzerland, Liechtenstein, Netherlands, Belgium, Austria, Vatican, USA, Canada, Dubai, Abu Dhabi, Malaysia,

Australia, New Zealand, Fiji, China, Japan, Thailand, South Africa, Singapore, Nepal, and Sri Lanka.

In the realm of scientific discovery, Dr. Nanda Nandan Das stands as a pioneer. He proposed a ground breaking theory explaining the Earth's rotation on its axis, resulting in day and night, as well as the Moon's revolution around the Earth, leading to the concept of a month. This theory, published in a magazine, was also presented to the Pathani Samanta Planetarium in Bhubaneswar, Odisha, providing valuable documentation. His innovating concept of existence of magnetic field in Earth and rotation of Earth on its axis have been sent to Peer Review for publication, which are yet the mystery.

Dr. Nanda Nandan Das's literary contributions are equally noteworthy, with 18 published books to his name. Notable works include "Letters to the Hon'ble Prime Minister PART-IA, PART-IB, PART-IC, PART-II, PART-III, PART-IV, PART-V, PART-VI, PART-VII, PART-VIII, PART-IX, PART-X (Twelve volumes)" which delves into administrative reforms in Bharat, and "Global Peace," a book that was sent to the Presidents/ Prime Ministers of about 170 countries during 2017. This effort led to significant diplomatic developments, including the meeting between the Presidents of America and North Korea in Singapore on June 12, 2018 on "Global Peace".

Dr. Nanda Nandan Das's devotion to social causes is also evident. He proposed the implementation of the Indian Citizenship Card to the Ministry of Home Affairs in 2009, a concept that later evolved into the Aadhaar Card. He tirelessly suggests innovative ideas to the Honourable Prime Minister of Bharat to create a crime and poverty-free nation. Additionally, he advocates for the inclusion of Moral Science, (Already suggested the course from class 1 to graduation, based on all being ideal Indians and how to make the country developed) in educational curricula and the reformation of the United Nations.

Dr. Nanda Nandan Das's ultimate aim is to foster patriotism, ingenuity, quality, and moral values among citizens, both in Bharat and globally. He envisions a world where countries function as a united family, and "Religion Humanity" takes precedence over any religious divide.

Throughout his tenure, Dr. Nanda Nandan Das initiated successful projects, such as installing statues of deities in government buildings to prevent disrespect. His dedication to service has been recognized by the national daily, Hindustan Times during 2002, among others.

The book "Letters to the Hon'ble Prime Minister" comprises a series of letters addressing critical issues. These letters touch on subjects like the Bharat-China border conflict, raising financial status, refunding chit fund investments, flood control, national education policy, and COVID-19's global impact, among others.

His entry in Universe, Earth, Country, State, District, Village:

1. The Universe: - Rotation of Earth on its axis forming day & night, existence of magnetic field on Earth, which are still remain mystery but have been discovered by Dr. Das.
2. The Earth: - His book GLOBAL PEACE had been sent to heads of 170 countries achieving peace globally.
3. The Country: - He initiated to introduce Indian ID card during 2009, the outcome is Aadhaar Card. Due to inspiration PM, Dr. Das suggested on many issues, which are included in 9 books of **'Letters to the Hon'ble Prime Minister'. Available-Amazon.**
4. The State: - OVERDRAFT of the state has been stopped due to his suggestion to Finance Minister during 2005.
5. The District: -He developed roads and new Rajghat Bridge.
6. The Village: - He developed road, school and Pravat Club.

This book **'Letters to the Hon'ble Prime Minister'** is a reservoir of instant solutions and a comprehensive encyclopaedia, dedicated to our beloved Motherland, Bharat.

Prof. Purnima Mitra,
Prof. NIIS group of Institution,
The Chief Editor.

CHAPTER I

HAPPY BIRTHDAY GREET

Your Grievance is registered successfully.
Registration Number: PMOPG/E/2024/0141428

HAPPY BIRTHDAY

Respected Narendra Modi Ji,
Hon'ble Prime Minister of India,

 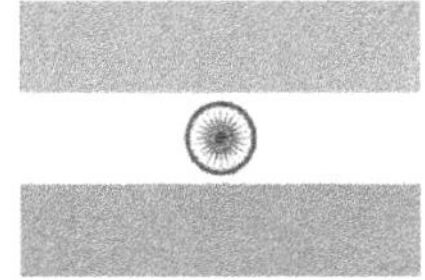

May God bless you with happiness and prosperity, and may you continue to lead with a vision for a Developed India and Global Peace.

 Happy Birthday to you.

Dr. Nanda Nandan Das, Original Thinker
Chairman, People's Welfare Suggestion Forum

Date: 17.09.2024

NARENDRA MODI, Prime Minister of India.
Date of Receipt-17/09/2024
Current Status-Case closed   -
Date of Action-18/09/2024
Reason-Others
Remarks-Sent to unit concerned.
Rating-Excellent

Rating

☆☆☆☆☆ Excellent

Rating Remarks   Satisfied

CHAPTER II

SAME RULES FOR BOTH MALES & FEMALES

Your grievance has been successfully.
Registration number: PMOPG/E/2025/0000623
Dt. 02.01.2025.
Respected Shri Narendra Modi Ji, Hon'ble Prime Minister of India,
I hope this message finds you well and in good spirits. The tragic suicide of Punit on 31.12.2024, due to conflict with his wife Manika, is a grave and sorrowful event. There must be a fruitful solution to prevent such tragedies. About a month ago, a similar incident occurred with Atul under almost the same circumstances.

Historically, sympathetic rules were created in favour of females due to harassment by some notorious males and criminals. However, this has inadvertently supported some ill-intentioned females in torturing males. Many innocent males have been wrongfully convicted due to harassment by females. Some females misuse these rules to torment their in-laws, citing dowries and other threats.

Therefore, it is requested to establish similar rules for both males and females. Nowadays, many females are earning well in business and service sectors, so the system should be equalized for both genders. In the worst cases, a narcotic method could be employed to ascertain the truth of any issue, with the involved personnel maintaining an impartial attitude.

With heartiest regards,
Yours sincerely,
Dr. Nanda Nandan Das, Original Thinker,
Chairman, People's Welfare Suggestion Forum
Dt. 02.01.2025.
Current Status-Case closed
Date of Action-03/01/2025
Remarks-Suggestion

CHAPTER III

ADDRESSING FALSE PROPAGANDA AND PROVOCATION

Registration Number: PMOPG/E/2025/0041403

Dt. 25.03.2025

Respected Narendra Modi Ji, Hon'ble Prime Minister of Bharat,

It has come to my attention that certain individuals, possibly affiliated with various political parties or minority communities, have been making unfounded statements. These claims, such as those alleging impacts on graveyards or religious institutions, seem intended to provoke and create divisions among the general public, particularly concerning the Wakf Board issue, related matters and different issues.

Such actions not only foster bias but also disrupt communal harmony. I humbly request that these individuals be held accountable and face legal consequences to deter the spread of false propaganda, whether during election campaigns or on other occasions.

With heartfelt regards,

Yours sincerely,

Dr. Nanda Nandan Das, Original Thinker

Chairman, People's Welfare Suggestion Forum

Dt. 25.03.2025

CHAPTER IV

WIDENING THE CHICKEN NECK OF EASTERN INDIA

Acknowledgement from the PM-

Your Grievance is registered successfully- Registration Number: PMOPG/E/2025/0026412

Respected Shri Narendra Modi Ji, Hon'ble Prime Minister of India, I am writing to address the urgent need for widening the 'Chicken Neck' in the eastern zone of our country. During the Bangladesh agitation last July and August 2024, there were distressing reports of Hindu and other communities being tortured, along with anti-Bharat sentiments being expressed. It was also mentioned that the eastern parts of Bharat could be separated, if the narrow strip of land between Bhutan and Bangladesh was captured. This narrow region poses a constant threat to the unity of our country as it is a weak point that could lead to the separation of Eastern Bharat. Some enemy countries are provoking Bangladesh to create agitation, potentially leading to the blockage of this crucial area.

I propose that this matter must not be ignored, and suitable steps should be taken to expand this narrow strip into a wider space, resembling the body of an elephant. By doing so, we can mitigate the threat and secure this vital region.

With heartiest regards,

Yours sincerely,

Dr. Nanda Nandan Das, Original Thinker

Former Secretary, Works Department, Govt. of Odisha

Chairman, People's Welfare Suggestion Forum

Dt. 24.02.2025

CHAPTER V

PROMPT ACTION OVER HEINOUS CRIMES

Your Grievance is registered successfully.
Registration Number: PMOPG/E/2025/0050590

Respected Shri Narendra Modi ji, Hon'ble Prime Minister of India,

Tahawwur Rana, a key figure in the 26/11 Mumbai attacks, has been extradited after nearly 17 years. It is worth noting that Ajmal Kasab, another terrorist involved in the same attack, was prosecuted over a span of four years, during which approximately ₹60 crore of public funds were expended.
Given the gravity of Rana's crimes, it is imperative that legal proceedings against him are expedited to avoid unnecessary delays and wastage of public resources. If required, existing legal frameworks should be reformed to ensure swift justice. With heartfelt regards,
Yours sincerely,
Dr. Nanda Nandan Das
Original Thinker
Chairman, People's Welfare Suggestion Forum
Dt. 11.04.2025

CHAPTER VI

VANTARA PROJECT, JAMNAGAR - A TYPICAL EXAMPLE FOR TOURING FACILITIES IN THE COUNTRY

Registration Number: PMOPG/E/2025/0030684
Date: 04.03.2025

Respected Shri Narendra Modi Ji, Hon'ble Prime Minister, India
I hope this letter finds you in good health and high spirits.
Certainly! Here's the edited part:
Your recent inauguration of the Vantara Zoo, as noticed on TV, highlighted an outstanding example of a modern zoo comparable to those in many developed countries. Such zoos would greatly enhance tourism facilities across the country, considering their feasibility. They would undoubtedly be significant sources of income.

In addition to the current attractions, incorporating various activities such as theatrical performances, water games, and dolphin shows, similar to those seen in many international destinations would further increase their appeal. Including lunch facilities in the ticket cost would provide a more comprehensive and satisfying experience for visitors.

These tourism facilities could be managed either by the government or through privatization. Such measures would not only generate substantial revenue but also contribute to the welfare of the animals, ensuring their proper nutrition, healthcare, and safety.

Furthermore, the successful implementation of the Vantara Zoo model across other regions could create numerous job opportunities, boost local economies, and position India as a top global destination for eco-tourism and wildlife conservation.
With heartiest regards,
Yours sincerely,
Dr. Nanda Nandan Das, Original Thinker
Former Secretary, Works Govt. of Odisha
Chairman, People's Welfare Suggestion Forum
Date: 04.03.2025

CHAPTER VII

STRATEGIC ACTION FOR SOLAR-POWERED ELECTRICITY

Registration Number: PMOPG/E/2025/0055289

Prompt Action on Adopting Solar Energy for Electricity Generation

Dt. 21.04.2024

Respected Shri Narendra Modi Ji, Hon'ble Prime Minister of Bharat,

On 10th April 2025, solar energy systems were installed in two nearby houses under a government-sponsored scheme. It was informed that a subsidy of ₹1,38,000 would be provided by the central and state governments for each installation. The total cost of installation for each unit is ₹2,20,000, which is paid outright.

This scheme is undoubtedly innovative and provides significant financial support to both the beneficiaries and the nation by promoting the generation of clean energy. Such a visionary initiative is a testament to your remarkable foresight in advancing sustainable energy solutions.

Post-installation, it was observed that each unit has the capacity to generate approximately 3 kW of electricity. The installation process was completed efficiently within two days, and the units were verified to produce 2.6 kW of power. However, there has been a significant delay in completing the paperwork required to connect the generated electricity to the respective households, leaving the process still pending.

This delay, which could potentially extend for months, results in a substantial loss of nearly 90 kW of solar energy per month per unit of installations. When viewed on a national scale, the restrictions on utilizing this solar energy exacerbate the overall loss, which is alarmingly high. Such wastage, caused by procedural inefficiencies, undermines the very purpose of this admirable initiative.

Additionally, the reimbursement of ₹1,38,000 to the beneficiaries has not been processed, and an unnecessary delay has been observed. It is imperative that the reimbursement process is scheduled within a clearly defined, time-bound period to ensure timely relief for the beneficiaries.

I humbly request your intervention to create awareness and streamline the process across all concerned departments. A maximum timeline of one week should be established to ensure that beneficiaries can utilize the generated solar energy promptly, it would be a big energy gain nationally. This would fulfil the scheme's objectives of immediate energy generation, timely financial relief, and efficient service delivery.

Furthermore, it is essential to establish a robust system for after-sales service and repairs. Accountability and responsibility should be clearly defined to address any defaults promptly.
With heartfelt regards,
Yours sincerely,
Dr. Nanda Nandan Das, Original Thinker,
Chairman, People's Welfare Suggestion Forum
Dt. 21.04.2024

CHAPTER VIII

PRESIDENT'S DECISION: POLICY FOR ALL

Registration Number: PMOPG/E/2025/0055810
Dt. 22.04.2025
Respected Shri Narendra Modi Ji, Hon'ble Prime Minister of Bharat, with heartfelt gratitude and deep respect, I submit the following suggestion for your kind consideration:
When a policy or bill is passed by the Lok Sabha, subsequently approved by the Rajya Sabha, and finally receives the assent of the Hon'ble President of Bharat, it reflects the will of the nation as expressed through its highest democratic institutions. Therefore, such policies, once fully enacted, should not be subject to further challenge in any court of law.
The Hon'ble Members of Parliament are the elected representatives of our 140 crore citizens, and the Hon'ble President of Bharat is the highest constitutional authority in the country. Once a policy receives Presidential assent, it becomes the law of the land and should be treated as a constitutional reference point for all institutions, including the judiciary.
Allowing such enacted policies to be challenged in court may undermine the constitutional supremacy of the Parliament and the President, and can be seen as contradictory to the democratic spirit and constitutional framework of our nation.
If no such legal protection currently exists to safeguard duly enacted policies from judicial review, I humbly propose that the necessary constitutional or legal amendments be considered to ensure that such cases are not admissible in courts. With deepest respect and warm regards,
Yours sincerely,
Dr. Nanda Nandan Das, Original Thinker
Former Secretary, Works Department, Government of Odisha
Chairman, People's Welfare Suggestion Forum
Dt. 22.04.2025

CHAPTER IX

ADDRESSING TERRORIST THREAT FROM PAKISTAN & A CALL FOR PEACE

Registration Number: PMOPG/E/2025/0064662
Dt. 08.05.2025

Respected Shri Narendra Modi Ji, Hon'ble Prime Minister of India For decades, Bharat has endured numerous terrorist attacks originating from Pakistan, the 'cursed nation', which has been the villain to put the whole world at unrest, in the name of religious terrorism. These terrorists, trained as suicide squads by their military, function as human ammunition, posing a grave threat to our national security. Tragically, our brave military, police, and security personnel have sacrificed their lives in the line of duty, resulting in not only irreparable human loss but also significant financial strain on the nation in terms of pensions and relief measures.

While eliminating terrorists provides momentary satisfaction, the underlying issue persists. Their military personnel remain untouched, ensuring the continuity of this cycle of violence. A strategic and comprehensive approach is necessary to address the root causes, safeguard our forces, and establish lasting peace in the region.

The missile attack through 'Operation Sindoor' on terrorist camps in Pakistan by Bharat on May 7, 2025, was undoubtedly a drastic step; however, the response by Pakistan's defence system should not be overlooked." The decision to give national honours to deceased terrorists from Pakistan has sparked controversy, with some viewing it as a sign of official support or connection between the country's defence establishment and terrorist groups. This move has raised concerns about the complexities of Pakistan's relationship with militant organizations and its implications for regional and global security.

Recently, General Asim Munir, the Chief of Defence in Pakistan, made statements that fuelled communal divisions between Hindus and Muslims. The tragic terrorist attack in Pahalgam, where Hindus were targeted for their Hindu identification and killed, appears to be a direct consequence of such rhetoric. This incident further underscores the disturbing reality that Pakistan's defence establishment harbours and facilitates terrorist activities.

It is evident that addressing terrorism alone is insufficient; a comprehensive approach is required to counter the deeper structural threats posed by Pakistan's defence apparatus. Strong measures must be taken to ensure national security and prevent such attacks from recurring.

Furthermore, Pakistan has suffered under mismanaged governance, leading to widespread poverty, crime, and terrorism. A nation plagued by instability cannot foster peace, as its education system, culture, and administration have encouraged extremism instead of harmony. The global community must recognize this reality and support efforts that promote a more stable and humane governance structure in the region.

Your leadership continues to inspire confidence in Bharat's security. We trust that decisive actions will be taken to safeguard our people and ensure long-term peace.

The undeniable truth is that all human beings are temporary inhabitants of this Earth, irrespective of religion or other differences. No faith can justify wrongful actions or provide refuge for harmful practices. Bharat stands as a testament to stability and harmony, despite its diversity, owing to its deep-rooted Sanatani culture, guided by principles such *Sarve Bhavantu Sukhinah* and *Vasudhaiva Kutumbakam*.

If Pakistan were to embrace values of humanity, grace, and environmental stewardship much like Bharat and integrate moral education inspired by Sanatani ideals, it would undoubtedly find a path to prosperity. These principles are not only vital for one nation, but they serve as a guiding philosophy for many countries plagued by violence and instability.

Your vision, exemplified during your G20 leadership under the theme "One Earth, One Family, One Future," resonates as the only viable path toward fostering a unified and ideal human society. History has shown that war-mongering, egoism, expansionist ambitions, terrorism, and religious conflicts have led to destruction and suffering, often

to consider my suggestions regarding necessary actions on Pakistan's defence activities while simultaneously fostering global awareness to combat war-mongering, ego-driven conflicts, expansionist policies, terrorism, and religious disputes. A unified effort in this direction can lead to lasting global peace.

Heartiest regards,

Yours sincerely,

Dr. Nanda Nandan Das, Original Thinker

Chairman, People's Welfare Suggestion Forum

Dt. 08.05.2025

The matter was debated in the Office of People's Welfare Suggestions on 08.05.2025 and presented for the awareness of the Hon'ble Prime Minister. The following members were present: Dr. Nanda Nandan Das, Er. Ambika Ballabha Swain, Er. Basanta Kumar Panigrahi, Santosh Kumar Naik, Seetakanta Das, Umakanta Jena and Lalmohan Murmu.

CHAPTER X

NATION BASED ON CRIME, TERRORISM: A CURSED COUNTRY

*(Santani culture shows a path to **PEACE**)*

Your Grievance is registered successfully.
Registration Number: PMOPG/E/2025/0063490

Dt. 05.05.2025
Respected Shri Narendra Modi Ji, Hon'ble Prime Minister of India,
The targeted killing of Hindus in Kashmir on April 22, 2025, in Pahalgam is deeply alarming for the Hindu community. Similar incidents in West Bengal and other parts of our country have raised serious concerns. The continuous attacks on Hindus and other communities by extremist groups have become an unsettling reality in certain nations.

Furthermore, recent remarks by Pakistan's army chief, Asim Munir, have sparked controversy for highlighting religious distinctions between Hindus and Muslims. Such statements from a defence leader risk deepening divisions and undermine the principles of inclusivity. Many critics argue that this reflects deeper challenges in the country's governance and approach to human rights.

THE TRUTH

Around 4.5 billion years ago, Earth separated from the Sun in a fiery state and gradually cooled over time. As temperatures dropped below 100°C, the cycle of life began. The earliest human-like animals appeared more than 100,000 years ago in Africa, gradually evolving and moving toward civilization over the past 10,000 years.

These nomadic groups spread across the world, forming distinct languages, religions, castes, and regional identities. As they settled, they defined borders for territories and nations based on their circumstances. However, fundamentally, all humans belong to Earth, and just like other living beings, they depart according to their destined time.

Religions emerged as guiding philosophies, and ethical systems were developed to provide structure and meaning. While the essence of most religious teachings focuses on the welfare of all, interpretations and writings often emphasize perspectives unique to each faith.

It has been observed that some countries uphold generosity and fairness by following the principles of their communities. However, misleading narratives have led extremist groups to manipulate their communities through false claims, bias, and provocation. As a result, targeted killings of Hindus and attacks on religious institutions have become alarming examples of this extremism. Furthermore, similar violence and persecution have been witnessed within communities across different nations.

Poor governance and negative administration have led to devastating consequences, mass killings, persecution of women, widespread poverty, crime, and terrorism, ultimately creating what can be described as 'Cursed Countries.'

Such extremist activities have triggered unrest in many parts of the world, posing a significant threat to global peace. At the time of independence, Pakistan (East & West) was designated as a Muslim nation to provide a homeland for Muslims while ensuring the well-being of minorities. India, despite having a Hindu majority, was established as a sovereign state. In 1976, the Preamble to the Constitution affirmed India's status as a secular nation. However, political strategies in subsequent years saw certain governments favouring particular religious communities for electoral gains through various amendments.

THE AIM OF SANATAN CULTURE

Sanatan culture is deeply virtuous, rooted in the noble principles of *Sarve Bhavantu Sukhinah* (may all be happy) and *Vasudhaiva Kutumbakam* (the world is one family). It promotes harmony among individuals, regardless of religious backgrounds, fostering a society based on mutual respect and peaceful coexistence. The integration of these Sanatani principles into Bharat's administration has contributed to the well-being of its people and the nation's progress.

During India's G-20 presidency, Shri Narendra Modi Ji emphasized the vision of *"One Earth, One Family, One Future."* This powerful statement reflects the foundational belief that all of humanity is interconnected, belonging to a single global family. It aligns with the essence of unity and collective well-being, reinforcing the idea that despite our differences, we share the same planet and a common destiny.

However, certain extremist groups in Bharat have resorted to divisive tactics, such as "vote jihad," with political parties utilizing them as vote banks. The targeted killings of Hindus in West Bengal, Kashmir, and other regions illustrate a disturbing trend that threatens social stability.

Despite Sanatan culture encompassing Hinduism, Sikhism, Buddhism, Jainism, and more being one of the oldest traditions in the world, there is no Hindu-majority nation globally. Therefore, the establishment of Bharat as a *Hindu Rashtra*, embracing the inclusive values of Sanatan culture, could serve to protect all communities.

Many devout individuals from various communities proudly identify as *Sanatani*, embracing their Bharatiya identity with deep reverence. Within this framework, all religious groups recognized as *Ideal Indians* would be encouraged to practice their faith within their respective institutions and homes, ensuring mutual respect and harmony without disrupting others.

The Concept of a Hindu Rashtra: A Framework for National Harmony

The proposed *Hindu Rashtra* would be guided by revised regulations applicable to all citizens, with the following measures:

1. **Preservation of Sanatan Culture** – Traditions that promote peace and do not harm any community should be upheld.
2. **Accountability for Provocation** – Individuals spreading false or inflammatory statements should face legal consequences, including restrictions on privileges.

3. **Strict Action Against Criminal Activities** – Offenses such as stone-pelting and bombing should be treated as attempted murder, with stringent penalties that exclude perpetrators from state benefits.
4. **Regulation of False Preaching** – Misleading religious or ideological teachings should be legally challenged to prevent misuse of freedom.
5. **Reforming Protest Mechanisms** – Open strikes and bandhs should be restricted, with protests channelled through elected representatives (MLAs and MPs) who would directly engage with the government.
6. **Promoting Ideological Harmony** – Communities engaged in falsehoods or provocations should be educated under a national policy that fosters unity.
7. **Judicial and Administrative Reforms** – Outdated laws causing delays and inefficiencies should be overhauled, with stronger enforcement mechanisms.
8. **Defamation of Bharat Abroad** – Citizens defaming the nation internationally should face consequences, including passport revocation.
9. **Safeguarding Sanatan Values** – Actions that undermine *Sanatan Dharma* should be restricted to preserve cultural integrity.
10. **Ensuring Public Decency** – The use of foul language in public discourse should be regulated.
11. **Equal Application of Laws** – Legal frameworks should be impartial and applicable to all citizens without discrimination.
12. **National Sovereignty Protections** – Supporting foreign entities that insult Bharat should be considered an act of treason.
13. **Addressing Electoral Misuse** – Voting practices that disrupt democratic balance, such as "vote jihad," should be prevented to ensure fair representation.
14. **Strengthening Security in Vulnerable Regions** – Jammu and Kashmir, due to security concerns, should remain a Union Territory, with voting rights reformed to safeguard Hindu cultural interests.

15. **Balancing Demographic Growth** – Measures should be considered within the voting system to ensure cultural equilibrium while maintaining inclusivity.
16. **Promoting Global Peace** – This initiative extends beyond national borders to contribute to worldwide harmony.
17. **Tourism and Development Conditions** – Investments in tourism and infrastructure should be contingent on the full security of Hindus in Kashmir.
18. **Universal Condemnation of Terrorism** – Terrorists threaten humanity and must be unequivocally denounced.
19. **Security Reinforcement in Kashmir** – The region should serve as a military and security training hub to eliminate terrorist networks.
20. **Sanatan Principles as a Global Solution** – The values of *Sanatan Dharma* can serve as a foundational approach to achieving international peace.

These points merit serious consideration for the broader interest of the nation.

With heartfelt regards,

Dr. Nanda Nandan Das, Original Thinker

Chairman, People's Welfare Suggestion Forum

Dt. 05.05.2025

NB: The matter was discussed in the office of People's Welfare

Suggestion Forum on 25.04.2025. The members present: Dr. Nanda Nandan Das, Er. Ambika Ballabha Swain, Uma Kanta Jena, Pramod Kumar Jena, Pranab Kumar Sahu, Er. Basanta Kumar Panigrahi, Santosh Kumar Nayak and Gayadhar Panda.

CHAPTER XI
INCLUSION OF MULTIPLE LANGUAGES IN EDUCATIONAL CURRICULUM

REGISTRATION NUMBER: PMOPG/E/2025/0028234
Dt. 27.02.2025

Respected Shri Narendra Modi Ji,
Hon'ble Prime Minister of India,
Despite having passed seven decades and more since independence, our educational system still faces moral and ethical challenges. One prominent issue is the linguistic diversity, resulting in challenges at the state level. Therefore, I propose the inclusion of a minimum of three languages in the educational curriculum of each state:

1. Hindi as the national language.
2. Local language of the respective state.
3. English as an international communication language.

These languages should emphasize moral values and similar concepts, using examples that reflect:

* The ideal Bharatiya spirit, with characters exemplifying honesty, sincerity, progressiveness, and creativity.
* Encouragement of mutual help and support among individuals.
* Self-sufficiency and income generation.
* Respect for religious customs within private and institutional spaces without disturbing others.
* Conducting public events with the permission of district administration.

INCLUSION OF MULTIOPLE LANGUAGES

* Uniformity in rules and regulations for everyone.

By implementing such a curriculum, we can foster a strong sense of nationality, morality, and unity among all citizens, ultimately strengthening the internal and external resilience of our country.

With heartiest regards,

Yours sincerely,

Dr. Nanda Nandan Das, Original Thinker,

Chairman, People's Welfare Suggestion Forum

Dt. 27.02.2024.

CHAPTER XII
SOLUTION TO THE DISPUTE BETWEEN DIFFERENT COMMUNITIES

Registration Number: PMOPG/E/2025/0034892

Dt. 12.03.2025

Respected Narendra Modi Ji, Hon'ble Prime Minister,

It has come to my attention that there is a dispute regarding the timing of Holi celebrations and Namaz prayers during the Holi festival. Similar issues have been resolved during other events. Unfortunately, there have been incidents of stone pelting while people were celebrating in front of mosques.

At the time of independence, East and West Pakistan were created to accommodate the majority Muslim population. There is not a single Hindu country in the world to perform and accommodate Hindu's culture. Despite assurances under the Nehru-Liaquat Pact that minorities in these countries would be protected, native Hindus and other communities have faced persecution.

India is a secular country, and it is essential to ensure that no community's practices create problems for others. All communities should be able to live comfortably without conflicts arising from religious practices.

Therefore, the other communities should consider adjusting their practices during festivals to avoid conflicts. In special cases, they may choose to observe their customs after special permission from the government. With heartiest regards,

Yours sincerely,

Dr. Nanda Nandan Das, Original Thinker

Chairman, People's Welfare Suggestion Forum

Dt. 12.03.2025

CHAPTER XIII
EXPANDING PEACE GLOBALLY

Registration Number: PMOPG/E/2025/0031361

Respected Shri Narendra Modi Ji, Hon'ble PM.

On 28th February 2025, a discussion took place between President Mr. Trump of the United States and President Mr. Zelensky of Ukraine. Unfortunately, the conversation concluded without any solution to derive peace.

Peace is essential for the survival of mankind. Here are some truths to consider for identifying individuals on Earth:

- After the Earth separated from the Sun in a burning condition, it cooled down, and after water accumulated, life began in water, on land, and in the air after crores of years.

- Human-like animals appeared more than hundreds of thousands of years ago and began to civilize due to the better fertility of their brains around ten thousand years ago. They spread across the world, creating languages, religions, castes, country borders, and many other differences. These are all human-made.

- These differences have led to egoism, the expansion of countries' borders, war mongering, terrorism, the forceful conquering of other countries, and massacres, resulting in the killing of natives and other communities. These actions destroy Mother Earth, promoting inhumanity, cruelty, crime, and terrorism. This is despite the fact that we all share the slogan of the Prime Minister of Bharat and Former President of the G20: "One Earth, One Family, and One Future," from the past session held in Bharat.

- The truth is that we all belong to Mother Earth and stay for a certain period. Nothing truly belongs to anyone, not properties, souls, breaths, or even our bodies. Therefore, the Mother Earth, where we have taken birth and stay, should not be damaged or destroyed by any means, whether through exploration, experimentation, or bombarding due to war and terrorism. It is the responsibility of all countries to prevent this. Such activities not only damage the Earth but also reduce its lifespan, which may be measured in millions of years, as there is a specific lifespan for all structures, living or lifeless.

- History shows that war is never beneficial for citizens or countries, whether they win or lose. It affects not only the involved countries but also the entire world globally.

- Therefore, the attitude of warmongering must be stopped by all means.

- Terrorists, who are demons in human form, must be strongly condemned.

- Crimes should be controlled through the strong enforcement of laws, similar to practices in Dubai, Singapore, and other countries. It can also be controlled through the moral values on humanity in the educational curriculum, which would generate ideal human beings globally.

- The minutes of the 107th session of the Thinker Club, debated internationally, vide Registration Number: PMOPG/E/2024/0174890, should be included as part of this issue.

- The United Nations should consider these points and modify the verdicts of 24th October 1945 to reflect the present situation.

I would like to present this issue to the UNO, if any instructions are necessary, please communicate these. I hope these points will be considered, and action will be taken from your end. With heartiest regards,

Yours sincerely,

Dr. Nanda Nandan Das, Original Thinker

Chairman, People's Welfare Suggestion Forum.

Dt. 05.03.2025

CHAPTER XIV
INCLUSION OF WORDS HONESTY, SINCERITY, PROGRESSIVENESS AND INNOVATIVENESS IN THE SWEARING SCRIPTS OF MINISTERS

Your Grievance is registered successfully.
Registration Number: PMOPG/E/2025/0019277

Dt. 10.02.2025
INCLUSION OF WORDS HONESTY, SINCERITY, PROGRESSIVENESS AND INNOVATIVENESS IN THE SWEARING SCRIPT OF MINISTERS

Respected Shri Narendra Modi Ji, Hon'ble Prime Minister, India

It is observed that even highly qualified individuals sometimes engage in corruption and criminal activities, often due to a lack of morality. If moral science had been a compulsory subject in the educational curriculum since independence, such a demoralized situation might have been avoided. During my visit to Japan, I was told by the guide, "Don't worry, if you leave something anywhere, it will remain untouched." Similarly, a driver in Norway told, "Please wait, let me pay the tax before driving." Such behaviour results from the moral values instilled in their education.

As Chairman of the People's Welfare Suggestion Forum, I have proposed introducing moral science as a compulsory subject to all Chief Ministers of the country and to your esteemed self through registration number: PMOPG/E/2019/0640330 - Dt. 01.11.2019. The products of such moral education would foster morality, unity, and a sense of national pride among all Indians.

Following the BJP's recent victory in Delhi, I have suggested several points for the development of Delhi under registration number: PMOPG/E/2025/0018684 Dt. 09.02.2025. I have recommended appointing two types of leaders and government authorities to ensure rapid progress while maintaining transparency: Excellent - honest, sincere, progressive, and innovative; and Outstanding - honest, sincere, and progressive.

Each government matter is overseen by a particular department, with the political head minister supported by the relevant government authorities. In addition to their excellence, the swearing script of ministers should include the words honesty, sincerity, progressiveness, and innovativeness. This practice should be adopted not only in Delhi state but also in all states and nationally as a regular oath. The inclusion of these words would serve as a constant reminder to the authorities to uphold their oath and be accountable for any violations. These four words should become a slogan for all government matters and among common citizens.

At the same time, all efforts should be made to introduce Moral Science (Registration number: PMOPG/E/2019/0640330) as a compulsory subject from class 1 to graduation in all types of educational curricula in the country, enriched with more ideal examples and rigorously reviewed by experts with a research mindset. This would stabilize morality, unity, and nationality, with a motive of 'country first' among all citizens, irrespective of differences. With heartiest regards,

Yours sincerely,

Dr. Nanda Nandan Das, Original Thinker,

Former Secretary Works, Government of Odisha,

Chairman, People's Welfare Suggestion Forum

Dt. 10.02.2025

CHAPTER XV
NO ENEMY MISSION FOR GLOBAL PEACE

Your Grievance is registered successfully.
Registration Number: PMOPG/E/2024/0163312

Dt. 06.11.2024
Subject: NO ENEMY MISSION TO ACHIEVE GLOBAL PEACE
Respected Shri Narendra Modi Ji, Hon'ble Prime Minister of India,

I am submitting the document titled NO ENEMY MISSION TO ACHIEVE GLOBAL PEACE (attached in PDF format) for your kind perusal and consideration. The document is self-explanatory, and I hope it aligns with your vision for promoting peace worldwide. I kindly request any steps that you may deem appropriate.

With the utmost respect and sincere regards,
Yours faithfully,
Dr. Nanda Nandan Das,
Original Thinker
Chairman People's Welfare Suggestion Forum

Dt. 06.11.2024
Date of Receipt-06/11/2024
Received By Ministry/Department-Prime Minister's Office
Grievance Document-Current Status-Grievance Received
Date of Action-06/11/2024
Officer Concerns To-Forwarded to-Prime Minister's Office
"No Enmity Mission"

NARENDRA MODI
PRIME MINISTER, INDIA

PEOPLE'S WELFARE SUGGESTION FORUM
COUNTRY FIRST

Regd. No.: 1567 / 2008 (Trust)
Bhubaneswar: Plot No. 2024, Chintamaniswar Colony, 751006, Odisha
Bhadrak-At Baudpur, Post- Madhab Nagar, Dist.- Bhadrak, Pin-756181-OdishaPh.: 9437617604, 9437312986
Email: nandanandan_das@yahoo.com

Dt. 06.11.2024

GLOBAL MISSION FOR PEACE THROUGH UNITY AND COOPERATION

Respected Shri Narendra Modi Ji, Hon'ble Prime Minister of Bharat,

The election of Donald Trump as President of the United States has created a renewed opportunity to strive for peace on Earth. Your previous cordial relations with President Trump could serve as a foundation for a continued partnership aimed at fostering global harmony. Bharat's positive diplomatic relationships with nations worldwide, including the recent resolution of issues on the LAC with China, further strengthen its position as a champion of peace.

As all humans belong to one global family sharing the same planet, we must recognize that divisions, whether based on religion, race, borders, or individual agendas, are artificial and harmful. These divisions often lead to enmity and conflict. Warfare, border tensions, and terrorism are products of outdated, narrow thinking, and should be discouraged through global awareness efforts. The enmity that exists between certain countries, often due to ignorance of shared humanity, could be addressed through a special "No Enmity Mission" that encourages mutual respect and understanding worldwide.

With this in mind, we propose the following principles as a foundation for global peace, aligned with the United Nations' mandate established on October 24, 1945, with necessary updates reflecting modern scientific advancements:

1. All human beings belong to one global family on Planet Earth.
2. Since life is finite, we must collaborate to promote peace and harmony, benefiting all.
3. Religion is a personal, social bond; individuals should freely practice their faith while respecting others.
4. National leaders should act as representatives within the United Nations framework, accountable for the well-being and development of their citizens.
5. The United Nations should oversee global defence systems to prevent international conflicts.
6. Nuclear energy should be utilized exclusively for space exploration, disaster management, and human welfare.
7. International decision-making should prioritize the consensus of the majority.
8. Educational systems worldwide should integrate a value-based curriculum emphasizing our shared human identity, transcending differences. (Value-based curricula promoting ideal human unity were sent to over 170 heads of state through the book *Global Peace* by Dr. Nanda Nandan Das.)
9. All forms of terrorism must be condemned and penalized with utmost severity.
10. The following principles (copyright of Dr. N.N. Das) should be universally acknowledged:

* Gods: The Sun, Earth, and our parents, as they sustain life.
* Religion: Humanity itself is the highest religion, as we are all members of the same human race.
* Caste: The only birth distinctions are male and female, with equal rights for all.

These points aim to unite humanity and create lasting peace globally. We urge for a comprehensive review of these suggestions and their potential implementation to build a harmonious and united world.

Thank you for your attention and support.

Warm regards,

Dr. Nanda Nandan Das, Original Thinker

Chairman, People's Welfare Suggestion Forum

Others' Support: Rtn Ambika Ballav Swain, Prasanta Sahu, Rtn Pranab Kumar Sahu, Prof. Purnima Mitra, Akhay Kumar Panda, Er Shree Nandan Das, Rtn Pramod Kumar Jena, Kumkum Das, Dr. Sachi Nandan Das.

Dt. 06.11.2024

Grievance Document

Current Status-Case closed

Date of Action-16/11/2024

Remarks: Your suggestions are always welcome. Should you have any other suggestions Register on MyGov App. You can Follow MyGov on Twitter/Subscribe to MyGov YouTube Channel also. Regards, CPIO MyGov

Rating

Rating Remarks   Satisfied

CHAPTER XVI

COPYRIGHTS AND PATENTS - PUBLISHED IN BOOK – LETTERS TO THE HON'BLE PRIME MINISTER.

COPY RIGHTS & PATENTS OF DR NANDA NANDAN DAS, THE AUTHOR

COPY RIGHTS:

1. GLOBAL PEACE.
2. LETTERS TO THE HON'BLE PRIME MINISTER.
3. LETTERS TO THE HON'BLE PRIME MINISTER Part IA.
4. LETTERS TO THE HON'BLE PRIME MINISTER Part IB.
5. LETTERS TO THE HON'BLE PRIME MINISTER Part IC
6. LETTERS TO THE HON'BLE PRIME MINISTER Part II.
7. LETTERS TO THE HON'BLE PRIME MINISTER Part III.
8. LETTERS TO THE HON'BLE PRIME MINISTER Part IV.
9. LETTERS TO THE HON'BLE PRIME MINISTER Part V.
10. LETTERS TO THE HON'BLE PRIME MINISTER Part VI.
11. LETTERS TO THE HON'BLE PRIME MINISTER Part VII.
12. LETTERS TO THE HON'BLE PRIME MINISTER Part VIII.
13. LETTERS TO THE HON'BLE PRIME MINISTER Part IX.
14. RELIGION HUMANITY
15. MANAV DHARMA (Odia).
16. JAGABHARATA BASI SAMAY KAM (Odia).
17. AMULYA RATNARA MALA.
18. MANAV DHARMA (Odia)
19. MAINTENANCE OF ROAD.
20. DISTRIBUTION OF L.C.
21. CONTROL OF OVERDRAFT.
22. COUNTRY AND STATES' DEVELOPMENT DEPEND ON GOVERNMENT.

23. INFORMATION TECHNOLOGY APPLICATIONS IN CIVIL ENGINEERING PROBLEMS.
24. BASIC PRINCIPLES ON ROAD-CONSTRUCTION.
25. HAPPY WAYS FOR HEALING NATURE.
26. ADOPTING DISASTER PROOFING TO CONSTRUCTION PROGRAMME OF WORKS.
27. RAMDAS BABAJI MAHARAJ O MAHATMA GANDHI.
28. ENGINEERING CHALLENGES IN DESIGN, EXECUTION AND MAINTENANCE OF ROAD.
29. THE EARTH FROM THE SPACE/PRUTHIBI BAHARU PRUTHIBI –Odia
30. NO SHADOW DAY AT BHUBANESWAR.
31. THE TRUTH OF HUMAN BEING
32. BRITAIN, JAPAN, ANDAMAN. INDIA-A HIDDEN HISTORY.
33. ADVERSE EFFECT OF VASTU SHASTRA.

PATENTS: -

1. ROTATION OF EARTH ALONG ITS AXIS & REVOLUTION OF MOON AROUND THE EARTH IN ANTI-CLOCK DIRECTION.
2. CONTROL OF ROAD ACCIDENT.
3. MAINTENANCE SCHEDULE FOR SAMBALPUR-ROURKELA ROAD, SH 10 –IMPROVED.
4. STRENGTHENING AND WIDENING OF SAMBALPUR-ROURKELA ROAD S.H-10
5. PREVENTIVE MEASURES TO FACE DISASTER.
6. CONSTRUCTION OF ROAD IN WATERLOGGED HIGHWAY STRETCH.
7. ROAD WITHOUT DRAIN A GREAT DISASTER.
8. ENGINEERING CHALLENGES IN COMPLETING PROJECTS TECHNICALLY AND TACTFULLY IN TIME.
9. PRINCIPLES ON CONSTRUCTION OF ROAD.
10. ENGINEERING CHALLENGES FOR SOLVING CRITICAL PROBLEMS ON ROAD PROJECTS:

11. PROBLEMS AND SUCCESSFUL SOLUTIONS FOR ROAD PROJECT.
12. ENGINEERING CHALLENGES SOLVING CRITICAL PROBLEMS OF FLOOD.
13. BUILDING: DEFECTS, PREVENTION AND REMEDIAL MEASURES.
14. CONSTRUCTION OF CYCLONE RESISTANCE BUILDINGS.
15. ENGINEERING CHALLENGES IN THE DESIGN AND EXECUTION OF BUILDINGS IN EXPANSIVE SOIL
16. CONSTRUCTION OF LEAK-PROOF ROOF WITH GREEN CONCRETE
17. EARTH FROM SPACE.
18. BUILDING POVERTY FREE ODISHA.
19. ORIENTATION OF HOUSE, NATURAL AIR CONDITIONING AND VASTU SHASTRA.
20. PREVENTIVE MEASURES FOR LONG LASTING HOUSES.
21. THREE STORIED BUILDINGS FOR EVERY INDIAN-NO MORE POVERTY.
22. IDEAL SMART CITY OF INTERNATIONAL STANDARD.
23. ENGINEERING CHALLENGES TO FACE CYCLONE, FLOOD AND DISASTER.
24. TYPICAL CONSTRUCTION- ANCHORED BUILDING.
25. PREVENTIVE MEASURES TO FACE DISASTER.
26. SOLUTION TO WATER LOGGING PROBLEM - TOURISM DEVELOPMENT FOR KONARK TEMPLE.
27. OUTSTANDING ENGINEER.
28. TACKLING FLOOD SITUATION IN VARANASI, MUMBAI AND PATNA.
29. MEASURES TO FACE DESTRUCTIVE SUPER CYCLONE AND FLOOD.
30. FALSE IS TRUTH FOR A MOMENT BUT FALSE FOREVER BUT TRUTH IS TRUTH FOREVER.

31. UNIVERSAL TRUTH.
32. INTRODUCTION OF MORAL SCIENCE FROM CLASS I TO GRADUATION.
33. THREE-D METHOD.
34. FIVE-M PRINCIPLE
35. NANDA'S SIX FORMULAE.
36. REAL GODS: SUN, EARTH and PARENTS.
37. RELIGION: HUMANITY.
38. CASTE: MALE & FEMALE.
39. I. OUTSTANDING, II. EXCEPTIONAL.
40. LESS TIME AND MORE WORK.
41. QUALITY OF OUTSTANDING OFFICERS.
42. NOBLE THOUGHTS.ADDITIONAL INNOVATIVE CONCEPT
43. CAUSE OF CREATION OF MAGNETIC FIELD ON EARTH-

It is still a Universal mystery. The author has discovered the reason of it and sent to PEER REVIEW for publication as per instruction from PM office Vide PMO registration number: PMOPG/E/2022/0217932 dt. 16.08.2022

NANDANANDAN DAS <nandanandan_das@yahoo.com>
To: prb-icsi@icsi.edu
Sun, Feb 19 at 3:49 PM -2023

Respected Sir,
I am Dr Nanda Nandan Das, Former E.I.C cum Secretary Works, Govt. of Odisha, PhD (Road), PhD (Building & Disaster). I have attached with this mail my original research on "REASON OF MAGNETIC FIELD ON EARTH".
I will be obligated and honoured if the esteemed ICSI panel members deem my paper fit for a peer review.
I have also attached the PU Questionnaire as mandated; I however would like to mention that I have written the paper from my individual capacity and not as an organization.
Thanks & Regards,
Dr Nanda Nandan Das

44. Entire universe is made of science. About hundreds of crores of years earlier, a mass got separated from Sun at left side in burning status by act of strong striking force over Sun. Such mass thrown up to far distance with revolving in anti-clock direction due to friction, became two parts. Bigger one is Earth rotating on its axis forming day & night and smaller one is Moon revolves around Earth in 28 days in anti-clock motion. After temperature reduced in course of time, the burning gaseous status of Earth became liquid lava, then after further cooled down, the top crust became solid with liquid volcano inside. After further cool down of temperature below 100* C, water accumulated and then life cycle in water, land, and air formed on Earth. Some lakhs of year earlier human look tailless creature appeared like chimpanzee and gorilla. Due to more fertility of brain, human beings became separate entity than other animals. They formed different languages, religions, castes, countries some truths for all:

1. All have taken birth on Earth. Human beings are a category among other living beings.
2. All will depart from the Earth.
3. Human beings are now social and like one family of the Earth.
4. Nothing belongs to any one, not even the body and soul, so all the times, do well for the family, society, country and the globe. We are guest to the Mother Earth.
5. GOD: -Sun, Earth and Parents.
6. RELIGION: - Humanity.
7. CASTE: -Male & Female.

These are completely new concept and recorded in the book GLOBAL PEACE, in chapter 'Global Peace', Chapter III of book LETTER TO THE HON'BLE PRIME MINISTER PART III and Chapter XXVII of book LETTER TO THE HON'BLE PRIME MINISTER PART IV, available through Notion Press and Amazon.

The above listed ideas are a testimony of the author's intuitive and exceptionally creative brain that has orchestrated engineering & social marvels, and brought laurels beyond the scope of an average brain to decipher.

CHAPTER XVII

CONTROL OF ROAD ACCIDENTS

Your Grievance is registered successfully.
Registration Number: PMOPG/E/2024/0179030

12.12.24   11:56 pm
CONTROL OF ROAD ACCIDENTS
Respected Shri Narendra Modi Ji, Hon'ble Prime Minister of India,
Today, on 12.12.2024, Mr. Nitin Gadkari, Hon'ble Minister of Transport, expressed sorrow in Parliament. Despite his efforts to develop India's communication system, he has been unable to control road accidents. He emphasized the need for public awareness.

In this regard, I would like to inform you that I have developed an innovative concept for controlling road accidents. This concept was published in "ENGINEERING CHALLENGES ON CONTROLLING ROAD ACCIDENTS (CASE STUDY)" in Vol. 41 No. 8 of Indian Highways (Special Number) during August 2013, and in the book "FINE TUNING OF ROAD AND BUILDING PROJECT - AN OUTCOME OF PRACTICE," available on Amazon.

I also suggested this concept to you via registration number PMOPG/E/2019/0658826 on 15.11.2019. The same is attached herewith for your kind perusal and forwarding to Mr. Nitin Gadkari, Hon'ble Minister of Transport for strong action to eradicate road accidents in the country.

If all the solutions to the causes of accidents are strictly followed by engineering departments, taught in engineering colleges, incorporated into public awareness through educational curriculum, and enforced by police and government, there would be no accidents, as Mr. Gadkari mentioned about Sweden. Drivers must be well-trained with special education and training, similar to many developed countries.

This is CHAPTER XXIX - CONTROL OF ROAD ACCIDENTS from my book "LETTERS TO THE HON'BLE PRIME MINISTER," already presented to you earlier.

THE BOOK IS A THINK TANK, COMPRISING INNOVATIVE AND ORIGINAL CONCEPTS BY THE AUTHOR, AN ORIGINAL THINKER, OFFERING SUGGESTIONS FOR MAKING BHARAT A DEVELOPED COUNTRY AND ACHIEVING GLOBAL PEACE.

With heartiest regards,

Yours sincerely,

Dr. Nanda Nandan Das, Original Thinker,

E. I. C & Secretary, Works Govt. of Odisha,

Chairman, People's Welfare Suggestion Forum.

Phone: +91 9437617604

Email: nandanandan_das@yahoo.com

Date: 12.12.2024

Attached- As above

CHAPTER XXIX- CONTROL OF ROAD ACCIDENTS

Dt. 15.11.2019- Registration number is: PMOPG/E/2019/0658826

SUGGESTED SCRIPT TO HON'BLE PRIME MINISTER, INDIA ON CONTROL OF ROAD ACCIDENTS

It is true that "Death is imminent" for any living being. But Death due to road accident is maximum for only human beings in our country. These are due to lack of awareness among common people and of government administration in the points covered in the paragraph "Primary Cause of Accidents on Road". There are various reasons for occurring road accident in the country. If all concerned authorities and people in general are careful and faithful to adopt the principles of road safety and abide by it, then the road accidents can be avoided. Author has taken care of all most all points considering from various angles and cited here for control of accidents on reality. He has put forth various means about safety on road as per actual performances during his long experience on different types of road projects. Due to deficiency and defects of road system major accidents occur, about which people are unaware of. Such points with remedies are indicated in the article, attached herewith. This has been published in IRC magazine and some items like small road junctions and drainage system, have been accepted by IRC. This is one of the chapters of my book "Fine Tuning of Road and Building Projects". It is believed that any award or publication, matters least. The main motive is the right implementation to prevent road accidents in totality, if such points get initiated. **With hearty regards,**

Dr Nanda Nandan Das, Original Thinker
Chairman, People's Welfare Suggestion Forum (PWSF)
Ex- Chairman, Gurujan Parishad
Former Secretary, Works, Government of Odisha
ENGINEERING CHALLENGES ON CONTROLLING ROAD ACCIDENT - (Case study)

ABSTRACT

It is true that "Death is imminent" for any living being. But Death due to road accident is maximum for only human beings in our country. These are due to lack of awareness among common people and of government administration in the points covered in the paragraph "Primary Cause of Accidents on Road". There are various reasons for occurring road accident in the country. If all concerned authorities and people in general are careful and faithful to adopt the principles of road safety and abide by it, then the road accidents can be avoided. Author has taken care of all most all points considering from various angles and cited here for control of accidents on reality. He has put forth various means about safety on road as per actual performances during his long experience on different types of road projects. The topic "Controlling Road accident-Road accident- Over view" put forth by Er Nandanandan Das, was critically discussed and approved by technical experts of works department of Government of Odisha during 2001. These have been circulated to all engineering departments as ideal guide as per the recommendation of the committee. Lot of methods for prevention of accidents have been codified by I.R.C for implementation but author has cited here in totality, considering the reasons of accidents and suitable remedies in general. These covers even measure existing I.R.C codes. These may be further analysed and detailed for covering better safety on road accidents.

1. INTRODUCTION

Role of road network system in the Country is known to everybody. Development of road system counts towards the development of the country. Now a lot of efforts have been taken for improving the road network system in the country. The speed of the vehicle can be maintained on road at 100 km/hr. There is sizeable increase of vehicles on transportation system in the country after independents.

It is noticed either road in bad condition or in good condition, accidents occur frequently. In our country traffic is mixed type. Different types of vehicles such as cycles, rickshaws, auto rickshaws, motor bikes, cars, tractors, trucks, buses, long tailors, even pedestrians etc. are allowed to pass on the road. That means road network system of India should be adopted, considering all these factors of mixed traffics. Generally, road accidents are occurred due to various reasons. When any accident occurs, people think, it is by chance or desire of God but there is particular cause for each and every accident. If cause of each accident is known, then the remedies for these can be adopted to avoid accidents

 It is observed although the speed, of vehicle is more than 140 km/hr in most of the developed countries, the accidents are less. Whereas although speed of vehicles is less in India, the number of accidents is more. Due to accident, there is a lot of damage of personal and national property, which also it leads to human loss. The place, where repeated accidents occur, are known as BLACK SPOT areas. If the types of accidents are known and remedial measures are taken suitably as antidote to treatment then, the lot of accidents can be avoided.

Primary Cause of accidents on road
- Due to bad driving.
- Due to drowsiness of driver.
- Due to mechanical trouble of vehicle.
- Due to carelessness by the traffic.
- Due to sudden entry of cattle, goats and other animals.
- Due to lack of civic sense of the traffic.
- Due to alcoholic & drug affect by drivers and pedestrians.
- Due to defectiveness of road / deficiencies in road systems.

2. REASONS OF ACCIDENTS AND REMEDIES IN DETAIL

2.1 Due to bad driving.

Many accidents are occurred due to driving of vehicles by the inexperienced drivers. Therefore, it is very much necessary to issue driving licenses, after proper driving tests. In no case driving licenses should be issued without proper driving test. In this respect both transport authorities and the drivers should maintain awareness because their slight slackness in this respect, will create a loss of life & property. In some countries in Europe the driving is one regular study like technical course.

2.2 Due to drowsiness of driver.

Many a time due to long driving, mostly after taking food, the driver feels fatigue, relaxed and drowsiness, which becomes the cause of accidents. When the driver feels drowsiness, he should take tea, brittle and should take rest for some time, before driving further.

On consultation with the police authorities, it has been noticed that in some particular time & area, the repeated accidents are occurred i.e. black spot areas, although there is no visibility of technical defects on road system. These are due to driving after taking food, feeling drowsiness after particular time. Locating such type of spots, the resting places, which should be provided on the side of road for taking rest by the drivers.

2.3 Due to mechanical trouble of vehicle.

Generally, the vehicles are not checked up or repaired periodically in our country for which usually accidents are occurred due to mechanical problems. Therefore, acts should be formed for periodical check-up for all vehicles. Periodical maintenance certificate should be obtained & produced whenever required by the R.T.O & police authority. It should be ensured that there should not be any slackness or irregularity while issuing such certificates.

2.4 Due to careless driving by the driver:

Many time the drivers drive the vehicles carelessly and become over confident for which a lot of accidents are occurred. In our country, everybody wants to go first. Therefore, when one finds a little gap between two vehicles, a driver tries to push in between, for which most of the accidents are occurred. These types of accidents   can be avoided   only by strict awareness   of the drivers. During driving of vehicles, the drivers should not use mobile phones, if it is very much required   to use phone, it is advisable to stop the vehicle on side for using the mobile phone. In no case the driver should be unmindful, superfluous and careless during   driving. In developed countries, generally the one driver gives indication to the other driver to go first. Therefore, although the vehicles in those countries like France, German, America and many other countries move very fast, the accidents are very less in compare to our country.

2.5   Due to sudden entry of cattle, goats and other animals.

At times when vehicles are moving fast, lot of accidents are occurred due to sudden entry of goats, dogs, cows, cats, bulls with fighting, child, cyclists, even other vehicles   & running of the person without   locating the traffic from the both sides. In developed countries generally grills, safety barriers, and guard rails etc. are provided to check against such type of accidents. In those countries' bulls, cows, goats and dogs etc. do not move on the road like our country. These animals are dealt separately. Sudden entry to the road is never advisable. For this awareness among the people is very much required.

2.6   Due to lack of civic sense of the traffic.

Generally, many accidents occur due to lack of civic sense. So civic of road traffic should be introduced from the   primary education of the child, to increase awareness for   use of road. The principles of movement of traffic in India are to keep to the left side of the road. Any fast-moving   vehicle while overtaking, should move on the right of the front   vehicle, provided the front vehicle has given indication to pass. When two vehicles are coming from different   directions, the 3rd vehicle should not   try to enter in between the gap.   Many a time if a truck is moving from one side and bus is coming   from   other   side, scooter   or cyclist tries to pass in between the gap for which accident happens on the road. This is only because of the impatience of the driver to go first. Many cycle riders carelessly during riding, face accidents. To go fast some motor cycle riders, move on the road zigzag way from one side to other side of the road locating gap in between the vehicles, create situation of accident. Many a times some friends move together on the road and they obstruct the road traffic   for which many   accidents also occur. They should move on the footpath at   the   left side edge as per the traffic rule. Therefore, the drivers should follow the traffic rule & indications which are given on the   road side sign board. The sign boards on   the roadside indicate the drivers to move   as per the situation of road. The drivers of different vehicles, moving on the road in same direction, should follow some safe distances in   between their vehicles and the vehicles in front, in order to avoid collision, if front vehicle applies brake in unavoidable circumstance. This gap is known   as   braking distance. This braking distance depends on different types of vehicles with different speeds moving of the road. This type of breaking distance can be indicated   on the side of road by the   traffic   authorities to grow awareness on the people.   These types of activities will reduce the possibility of accident.

In Parish and border of Italy there was an accident of burning of a petrol bunker on 24th March 1999 inside a tunnel (11.6km) in "Mont Blanc". Due to this there were 39 death and 10 cars with 23 lorries were damaged. Subsequently it was codified to maintain the safe distance of 100m in between the front and rear vehicle inside the tunnel.

When both the gates are closed in any railway level crossing, it is usual practice to cover both side lanes on both sides of gates by the traffic. These are due to lack of common sense of drivers. For this unnecessary jam is created after opening of the gates. In developed countries, the drivers follow the traffic rule strictly.

In India suppose by chance any vehicle becomes   out of order and stuck on the road, usually both lanes are covered with both way traffic, for which jam is created. These are all due to lack of common sense and awareness. In this case the traffic on left side lane should be used and other side should be left vacant for incoming of other side vehicles to avoid jam.

2.7   Effect of alcoholic and   drugs on drivers and also pedestrians.

On principle, none should drive the vehicle after taking alcohol or drug. One must realize any accident occurs due to one's such activities, it is harmful to individual as well as to all. Similarly, a drunkard while moving on the road may lose his sense and meet accident, so the pedestrians   must not move on the   road as drunkard or using drug. Police must be very much active to check on the matter and take immediate action over it. Driver should always remember that the life of passengers and the vehicles depends on his type of driving.

2.8   Due to deficiency or defectiveness of construction of road system.

Major accident is occurred due to defect of road or deficiency of road construction system. Generally, about the 60% accidents are occurred due to deficiency in road system. These type accidents happen due to technical ignorance or by the negligence of the concerned engineers during execution of road work. If any accident occurs, general opinion of the common people is that these happen by chance or it is desire of God.

 The road network system is different, location wise. The road system of Odisha is not same as Darjeeling, Simla, even Rajasthan. Such difference on road system depends on longitude, latitude, forest area, hilly area, desert, coastal area, water logging area, cyclone and flood affected area etc. Actually, the road policy of Indian Road Congress is adopted all though the country. The constructional method of road system should be adopted as per the situation and environment all over the country. Some precautionary measures on road accidents have been adopted in real practice in the State of Odisha. The same have been cited here in detail item wise.

PARTICULAR METHODS FOR AVOIDING ACCIDENTS ON ROAD:

2.8.1   Where in any town or market area, road and the road side land are mostly in same level for which random entry of cross traffic like cyclist, motor cyclist, running of different persons on road cross wise create accident on the road. It is suitable to provide grill or pedestrians guard rail (PGR) to restrict the random entry of the traffic. Another method for separating the road from the road side land, provision of V-type drains is recommended. These will restrict the sudden entry of cross traffic to the road. This will minimize the accident on road. A typical section vides Fig-I - As road safety measure: -

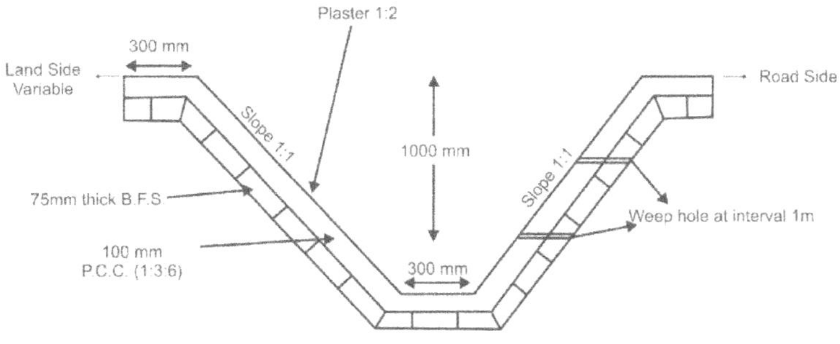

Fig-1

The drain should continue from the formation edge of the road. Guard posts should be fixed to identify the edge of road. Due to such type of drain, accident also minimize in town, market and village areas. It restricts the random entry of traffic from the adjacent land or locality to road directly. At restricted places passage should be provided for entry of local traffic. The Hume pipe culverts may be provided in suitable locations with sufficient width so that the traffic coming from the outer to inner side of road can see the traffic from the both ways on the main road. This was adopted in places like Kansara, Jalan petrol pump, Rajanpur, Jharsuguda, Hedayas etc. and found success in Sambalpur - Rourkela Road.

There are three types of advantages for adopting such V- type of drain.

2.8.1.1 This type of drain acts as prevention of accidents.

2.8.1.2 During rainy days due to rise of water table inside the ground, generally there is ingress of water from neighbouring land to inside of the road and there will be vertical action of water pressure under bottom of road. Provision of such type of drain acts as cut off between road and side land. This has been adopted practically in Sambalpur –Rourkela Road (SH10) and found successful.

2.8.1.3 This drain also carries the storm water from the road and also from road side land. Therefore, road is better maintained.

2.8.2 Mostly in curve and junction of road, the clear sight distance is to be maintained. Therefore, any structure or plantation of tree should not be there inside of the curve because these obstruct the sight distance, that means there will not be clear vision either during running and over turning. The building and plants may be in outer side of the curve.

2.8.3 Humps of the road create inconvenient for the flow of traffic. At times the humps are of abnormal size for which many accidents occur. Humps are provided for checking the speed of vehicle. These are mostly near any road crossing and school area. Generally, in many locations, the humps are provided on road due to repeated accidents, already occurred. If one tries to find causes of accident, it would be noticed that there must be one cross road connecting the main road. The reasons of accident may due various causes, such as Cross road meet the main road in steep grade, there must be lot of structures, betel shops and trees at turning places, which obstruct the sight distance. The traffic coming from the cross road, meet accident on the main road for which generally humps are provided on the main road to avoid such accident. A typical road junction as per figure-2 is suggested as remedial measure. There should be curve entry from connecting road to main road. There should not be any obstacles on the curve side to have proper sight distance. Instead of providing humps on main road, ramblers should be provided at a distance of 10M as per the standard and that should be on the cross road. The rumblers should be extended from edge to edge on connecting road. No cross traffic should enter the main road with high speed. Rather, these traffics should be cautious while entering to main road.

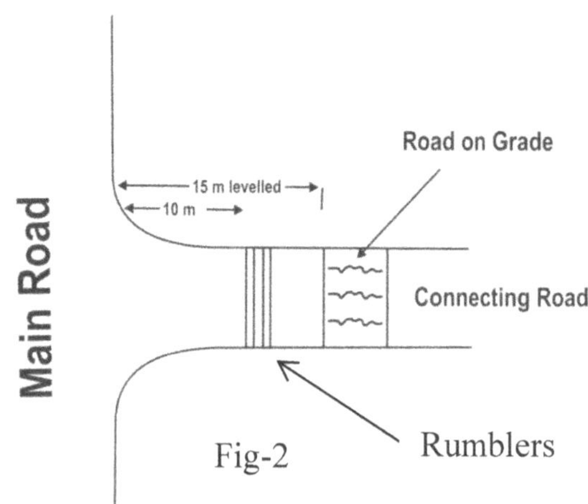

Fig-2

Therefore, the level   of connecting road should be maintained as per the level of edge of main road, providing proper camber on the levelled part of such road for a length of 15 meters and after which road should negotiate with exiting road in grade. To provide such type of junction on the road, all the engineering departments   of government of Odisha   have been intimated   as an ideal guide to restrict the accident. Author had given lot of proposals on improvement on road to CGM, NHIA during 2005, it is very much well coming that the very typical method has already been adopted in small road crossing in the road system.

2.8.4   Changing the direction of road in closer interval should be avoided to minimize the accident.

2.8.5   Due to carelessness in providing transition between the curve and straight edge of the road near Sundar gad in SH10, there were a lot of accidents. Therefore, transition should be as per the proper design and proper super elevation should be provided in transition portion. Lacking of proper slope in transit portion has caused lot of accident as experienced.

2.8.6   Direct grade should not be ended on the junction of the road and also   approaches of bridges and culverts, rather suitable grade can be adopted after maintaining the levelled approaches for a length of minimum 15m.

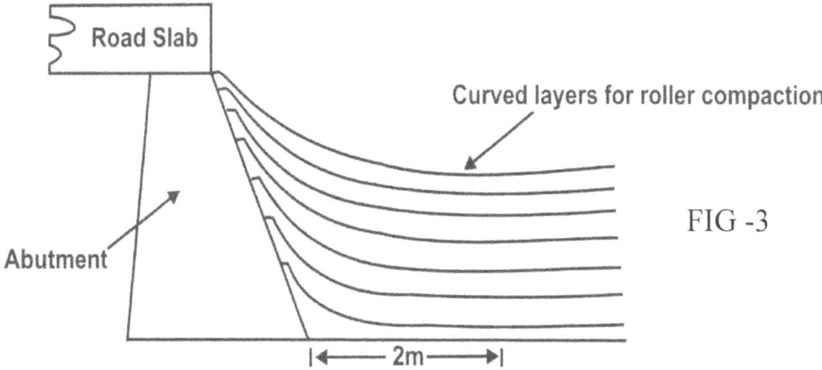

Generally, it is noticed that the joint of culvert and starting of approach of road is settled, for   which lots of accidents and inconvenience on movement of traffic are occurred. This is due to under compaction of approach near abutment. The earth work from the first layer and in subsequent layers should be bent vertically towards abutment so that the compaction by roller can be made properly on the edge of abutment. The typical section as per Fig-3, indicates the method of compaction layer wise.

2.8.7   During improvement of Rourkela and Sambalpur Road, lots of road furniture such as sign board, delineators, etc. were put on the side of road. These items were very precious, as per international standard. It was observed that after some days the road furniture were stolen and broken by the miscreants. This furniture was visible at night. But after stolen of materials, the cheap type of furniture was used for which the position of furniture was not visible during night. Therefore, number of accidents increased. These should be insured against theft and damage.

2.8.8   Super elevation should be provided as per the design of curve. The slope of Super elevation should be from inner to outer edge of the curve. Super elevation on curve part of road, was inner edge of curve to outer edge of carriage way and outer shoulder was in camber in Sambalpur-Rourkela Road. Therefore, there were lot of accidents, while crossing of third vehicle on the upper shoulder by chance. This was rectified on the remedial measure in road accident in the state of Odisha. Of course, providing slope from inner to outer edge in curve part of road has been codified in I.R.C standard. Such type of slope should be maintained in transition part also. Providing the slope in super elevation depends on type of curve with its radius of curvature. Due to non-provision of proper super elevation in any curve there is possibility of accident. Guard posts should be provided in curve and transition part of the road which will indicate the existence of curve.

2.8.9   It is desirable to have road side plantation, therefore it is always advisable to retain one side trees of the road at the time of widening the road.

2.8.10 If the number of curves is more in closer interval, the possibility of road accidents increases. More number of curves increase the length of road. For which the time period covering the more length of road increases and also the maintenance expenditure becomes more. It is seen generally roads are improved on existing road which are having number of curves to avoid land acquisition. On the other hand, comparing the cost, improvement of existing road with a greater number of curves to new straight road with land acquisitions may be more. Therefore, only unavoidable curves should be allowed during improvement of road.

2.8.11 It was experienced that the delineators used in Sambalpur-Rourkela-SH10 were no doubt very much welcoming but these were stolen and damaged due to activities of miscreants later on. The fruitful purpose of proving delineator was unsuccessful and a greater number of accidents occurred. Subsequently these were replaced by guard posts with reflecting paint. Therefore, guard posts may be used in place of delineators as per the situation.

2.8.12 When the road is passing through congested area, grill on both side of road may be provided to restrict random entry of cross traffic. If more width of land is available, the main road can be elevated above 1m height and service road on both sides can be provided to allow local traffic as   grade   separator. This will reduce jam and will be economical.

2.8.13 Sudden rise and fall of road vertically, creates accident. Step should be taken to avoid it.

2.8.14 Odisha is one flood and cyclone affected area. During 1999 due to super cyclone and flood, most of the roads were submerged in water and roads were damaged. Therefore, height of road should always be higher than the H.F.L. The bridges and culverts   should have sufficient vantage to accumulate flood discharge. This will minimize flood on road. It is experienced during cyclone of 1999 that the falling of trees on the road created problem for transportation of essential communities. Even, falling of big plants damage the electric and phone lines. Therefore, plantation of small   verities of trees of maximum height 5m should be planted at 3m away from edge of road formation, so that the falling of trees by cyclone will not obstruct the traffic nor create any hindrance for transportation of essential commodities. The electric and phone lines should be always away plantation line.

2.8.15 It is not desirable to plant the fruit bearing trees near   side of the road. Because the people generally will be interested to use different means to get fruits for which there will be disturbance of the movement of traffic. Small verities of trees like Aashiya, Crunched, Baula, Karanja, small verities of Neem and such other similar type of plants of height within 5m should be planted at a distance of 3m from road. Same variety of plants   should not be planted for a longer stretch. Because this may create monotony to driver while moving   on the road for a longer stretch. This monotony at time creates accident. Therefore, it is advisable to plant trees of same variety for   a stretch   of three kilometres maximum, by which the monotony on driving will be minimized.

2.8.16 Due to lack of proper maintenance of road, in many places, the shoulders on both sides of carriage way, are washed out which create pot holes and undulation on shoulder and creates level difference on road. This becomes cause of accident. Therefore, care should be taken to level the shoulders with proper camber by using earth or murmu and compacting by roller   properly.

2.8.17 The width of road should be maintained same through out to avoid accident.

2.8.18 It is seen that there   are trees, electric line, phone line etc. on the road within road formation edge for which lots of accidents are occurred. Therefore, such type of any structure should not on road.

2.8.19 In two lane road, having heavy   movement of traffic and if there   is   availability   of sufficient width of road, then the road should be made four lanes with   provision of median as per the design standard. Since   there will be flow of traffic from both of sides separately, accident can be avoided.

2.8.20 Road side   light arrangement   should be made for proper vision at night. Now a days the lighting arrangement by solar energy system can be used for illumination at night.

2.8.21 The   existing narrow bridges and culverts should be widened and   extra lanes may be provided to accommodate the present traffic.   While proceeding from wide road to narrow bridges and culverts guard posts at intervals   should be fixed to indicate the narrow   approach toward the bridge. Reflecting paints should be marked on the guard post, so   that this will be visible at night. Road also be painted with reflecting marking. These indicate the border of carriage ways.

2.8.22 Generally, it observed due to parking of different vehicles, such as trucks, buses, cars, tractors and motor cycle on the road, traffic congestion is created, which is also cause of accident. Therefore, suitable parking places should be provided at interval to avoid such problems.

2.8.23 In our country there are mixed traffic such as cyclist, rickshaw, motor bike, tempo, tractor, truck, bus etc. Therefore, road marking with different indications should be made to segregate the different traffics. Pedestrians should walk on foot path only.

2.8.24 Lot of accidents are occurred due to advisement hoarding in different places of road. This diverts the attention of drivers. Therefore, the hoarding may only be provided where these will not divert the attention of drivers.

2.8.25 It is observed in many places the black toping part of road is found very smooth. It is due to excessive contain of bitumen in bituminous layer. During hot season due to melting of bitumen huge bleeding on the road surface is found. It seems as if road is in very good condition. Due to smoothness of road, there is less friction effect on vehicle on the road. So, at the time of requirement of brake the vehicle sleeps and at time meets with accident. When there is slight rain, the moisture contains on the road acts as viscous, therefore the vehicle loses friction effect and tends to meet accident. Author had experienced of one such type of accident in NH6 near Chhatabar, Odisha in similar principle. Precautionary measures should be taken to avoid use of excess of bitumen during construction of road.

2.8.26 Accidents in hilly areas is usual matter, since most of the hilly roads are narrow and not as per the design standard. Therefore, the hilly roads should be properly designed to avoid such accident. The well-trained drivers should be allowed to move in such hilly area.

2.8.27 Besides engineering measures, there is a need for traffic regulation and proper education of the road users. The driving silence system should be more rigorous. Facility should be provided for imparted proper training to the drivers. Registration to only road worthy vehicles should only be renewed.

2.8.28 Traffic regulation should be strictly introduced in educating the lower age group to develop civics sense in general.

3. CONCLUSION:

An analysis of accident data indicates that not only driver's fault but also public carelessness is mainly responsible for the majority of the accidents and fatalities. Studies undertaken abroad have revealed that reduction in accidents to the extent of 20 percent is possible by taking recourse of proper engineering measures through planning, design, construction and maintenance of roads. An accident-prone spot i.e. black spot areas may be identified and separate fund may be created out of the motor vehicle taxes for improvement of the accident-prone spots.

Proper and detailed data on accidents are not available in our country. It is being collected by police from their view point. The transport department collects accident statistics involving their transport corporation vehicles. Therefore, a separate Road safety cell, consisting of Engineer, Police, Transport, Local representative, Concerned NGOs, should be created. The name of the cell may be named as "NATIONAL INTEGRATED ROAD SAFETY CELL" (NIRSC). They should be responsibility for collecting and analysing data of all accidents and making specific recommendations for averting accidents. To reduce frequency of accidents, the data regarding type of accidents (i.e. motorized or non-motorized), specific months and days of accidents, maximum types of vehicles involved, reason of accident, fatality rate, difference in occurrence of road accidents before and after creation of Traffic Aid Post if any, etc. may be collected from accident prone location. Since, the geometric design of the highway has a direct effect on accident rate both in terms of number and severity, the design of various road elements like vertical profile, horizontal alignment, cross sectional features should take in to account the road safety measures.

Author had experienced in working in Daitary to Paradeep port (Express way project) in Odisha from 1965 to 1975 and in charge of Sambalpur to Rourkela Road, ADB project from 1996 to 1999. The above possible data have been arrived out of a long experience and many are found successful on execution. All possible efforts have been made to cover the possibility of accidents. Further detailing in many points are required to overcome some type of accidents. Little care during execution can avoid many accidents. In India the road policy is adopted as per guide line of IRC. There are still lots of data yet to be included in IRC standard, which have not been reported by experienced engineers.

The "ENGINEERING CHALLENGES ON CONTROLLING ROAD ACCIDENT (CASE STUDY) HAS BEEN CIRCULATED

LETTERS TO THE HON'BLE PRIME MINISTER, PART- IX

IN THE VOL.41 NO. 8 OF INDIAN HIGHWAYS (Special Number) DURING AUGUST 2013 AND
PUBLISHED IN THE BOOK" FINE TUNING OF ROAD ANDBUILDING PROJECT-AN OUT COME OF PRACTICE".
Dr. Nanda Nandan Das
Former E.I.C and Secretary, Works, Government of Odisha
Ph-9437617604
Dt.15.11.2019

भारतीय राष्ट्रीय राजमार्ग प्राधिकरण
(सड़क परिवहन और राजमार्ग मंत्रालय, भारत सरकार)
National Highways Authority of India
(Ministry of Road Transport & Highways, Govt of India)
क्षेत्रीय कार्यालय, ओड़िशा /Regional Office, Odisha
301 - ए, तीसरी मंजिल, पाल हाईटस, प्लाट् नं जे/ 7, जयदेव विहार, भुवनेश्वर - 751013, ओड़िशा
301-A, 3rd Floor, Pal Heights, Plot No : J/7, Jayadev Vihar, Bhubaneswar- 751013, Odisha
दूरभाष /Ph.: 0674 - 2361470/ 570/670 (कार्या)
ई-मेल/e-mail : roodisha@nhai.org, ronhaiodisha@gmail.com, वेबसाइट/Web : www.nhai.gov.in

NHAI/13011/13/RO/OD/ **62** /2024   09.01.2025

To.

    Shri Nanda Nandan Das
    Plot-2024, Chintamaniswar
    Bhubaneswar, Khordha
    Odisha

Sub: Public Grievance pending at CPGRAMS portal ID-reg.

Ref- 1. PMOPG/E2024/0179030 dated 12.12.2024

Sir,

    Please refer to your PG Registration no- PMOPG/E2024/0179030 dated- 12.12.2024 where you have given some suggestion based on "Engineering Challenges on controlling Road Accident (Case study) in vol 41 No. 8 of Indian Highways during August 2023.

2.   In this regard, it is to inform that NHAI is taking all necessary safety/engineering measures for controlling Road accident as per MORTH specification & IRC guideline .

Yours sincerely,

(Amit Kumar Gupta)
Dy. General Manager (Tech)

Current Status=Case closed **Date of Action**=13/01/2025
Remarks-Reply attached.
Officer Name=Sh. S.K Patel (GM HR Admn Coord), NHAI.

CHAPTER XVIII

LESS TIME BUT MORE WORK

(Copy Right of Dr. Nanda Nandan Das, Original Thinker, the Author)

Your Grievance Registration Number: PMOPG/E/2025/0005136

Dt. 11.01.2025

Respected Shri Narendra Modi Ji, Hon'ble Prime Minister
of India,

I hope this message finds you in good health and spirit. I attach herewith my original thoughts on the life of the human mass, focusing on building careers to become ideal citizens with 'Outstanding' and 'Exceptional' character, embodying morality, unity, and nationality. Such citizens can be catalysts for building a developed country and bringing global peace. This innovative concept can be scrutinized by experts with a research mind-set, and planning can be made to build a developed country and achieve global peace.

This version must reach our esteemed Prime Minister, Shri Narendra Modi Ji.

With heartiest regards,

Yours sincerely,

Dr. Nanda Nandan Das, Original Thinker

Former Secretary, Works Govt. of Odisha

Chairman, People's Welfare Suggestion Forum

Former Chairman, Odisha Durneeti Sangharsa Mancha

Dt. 11.01.2025

LESS TIME BUT MORE WORK

(Copy Right of Dr. Nanda Nandan Das, Original Thinker, the Author)

Earth is the only planet in our solar system, where life exists. Nothing here is permanent. Just as the soul enters the body, it must leave one day, because the Earth belongs to no one. For example, when somebody travels by train, the berth is reserved for the person until the train reaches the destination, but the train does not belong to the person. Similarly, when one visits a cinema, the seat is reserved for the person until the end of the film, but the cinema hall does not belong to the person. Likewise, a person may own land and buildings on Earth and enjoy them as long as they live, but the Earth does not belong to them.

Humans are more sensible than other animals. When the Almighty sends human beings to Earth, they should only do good things here. Whether one's stay is 30 years, 50 years, or 80 years, life is short. Therefore, everyone should avoid cheating, injustice, corruption, crime and terrorism. Instead, be good speak the truth, help others, and be honest, sincere, and hardworking. If such principles are adopted by everyone, we can see a developed society, state, and country, which will lead to global peace.

Any passenger sitting inside a train must get down at their destined station. Getting down at an earlier or later station does not depend on how old the passenger is. A young person may get down at an earlier station than an older person. Nobody knows the last day of their life, but this is true. Therefore, the thought that one is young and will do good things later in life is undesirable.

The period from birth to death can be considered in four stages:

1. First stage: From birth to starting of study.
2. Second stage: Starting of studies to completion of studies.

3. Third stage: Beginning of service or business to retirement or attending the age around 60 years.
4. Fourth stage: After retirement until waiting for last day.

All should keep in mind the following "Universal Truth":
- We have not come to Earth Suo- motto.
- The Almighty has sent us here.
- This Earth does not belong to us.
- We are here for a certain time.
- So long as we are here, let us do only good work.
- This is the desire of the Almighty.
- We do not carry anything when we depart from Earth.

Like the mosquito, fly, tiger, dog, fish, etc., human beings are living creatures. Since human beings are intelligent among others, we are able to make plans and understand the universe. Everyone knows that if there is birth, there is death. It is like appearing on a stage for some time and then going back to the green room.

The lifespan of a dog is about 15 years that of an elephant is about 70 to 80 years. Some insects live for only a few days, while rats may live up to 4 years. Similarly, the lifespan of a human being is about 70 to 80 years. Generally, people who live past 80 years, lose their mental faculties. This life period is very short compared to the age of the Earth. Even fossilization, such as a plant turning into stone, may take more than millions of years. In comparison, human life is very short. Some Super power has sent us here, desires that we achieve some good work in our lifetime. Therefore, as long as we are here, we should think good and do well instead of thinking ill of others. This is the desire of Almighty.

Whether in business or government service, if one performs their duty with honesty and sincerity for the benefit of society, then their existence on Earth will be fruitful. Generally, we see people after committing irregularities, dishonesty, even crimes, and then going to religious places to atone for their faults, thinking that the religious work will help them in the next birth. They do not know, if there is a next birth or not. If a person does good work sincerely and with honesty, then one will be definitely successful.

Since the Almighty has sent us here, we can only fulfil the desire of the Almighty in the following manner:

* Always speak the truth. Never speak falsehood. "Falsehood is truth for a moment but false forever, while truth is truth forever."
* Be very sincere in your duty and never cheat.
* Be honest and never be involved in corruption or theft.
* Never do any work that will harm others.
* When discussing a matter, adopt the 3D methods: (1) Discussion, (2) Debate, and (3) Decision. Individuals should put forth their suggestions, and a fruitful decision can be achieved.
* Be smart and sober.
* Never take any decision after hearing only one side. Always think of yourself as a judge and decide accordingly.
* Never make mistakes.
* Always follow a pre-planned schedule for work to have a good family life and successful professional life.
* Time is the essence of life. It never waits for anybody. Many reach a program late, thinking it will create more importance, but this is incorrect and considered slackness and laziness.
* Always remember that we have come to Earth for a very short time, even if it is hundred years, and we should strive to do the best work possible in that short time. This is the desire of God.
* Without being overly involved in religion, if one works sincerely, God will always support them.

LESS TIME BUT MORE WORK

BRIEF OF FOUR STAGES OF LIFE:

1.   First Stage: This period is from birth to the start of study. During this time, much care should be taken of babies. They should be properly trained on how to deal with family and society. Babies should always be cheerful. Never tell babies false words, use bad language, or treat others poorly because this reflects on the baby. Good training leads to becoming a good citizen of the country. Babies should always be kept away from bad habits, behaviour, and environments.

2.   Second Stage: This stage is from the start of study to completion of study. Students should follow discipline, give importance to their studies, and always speak the truth. They should complete their homework before going to school. They should also participate in play, drill, and other school activities. Students should plan for the next day, behave well with friends, teachers, parents, and others, and stay informed through TV, radio, and newspapers. They should accept good things from any religion and view everyone as human beings, not through the lens of different religions or castes. Never think ill of others or allow injustice. Dedicate themselves to studies and memorize lessons through sincere study. Students should be smart and sober and discuss good thoughts with friends and teachers, exchanging ideas. They should limit extra expenditures and avoid bad habits like chewing betel, or smoking cigarettes, as these habits are harmful to health and finances. For example, if a person drinks tea costing Rs. 10.00 a day, it totals Rs. 300.00 a month, Rs. 3600.00 a year, Rs. 36000.00 in 10 years, and Rs. 1, 80,000.00 over 50 years. This amount could be spent on some constructive work, nutritious food to improve strength, body, and mind.

To create good habits in students, moral science should be a compulsory subject from Class 1 to graduation. Before obtaining a degree, students should undergo military training during the summer course of their graduation period to instil bravery. Such a course of moral science has been prepared after debates with educationists and intellectuals. It has been suggested to the Hon'ble

Prime Minister of India in letter number: PMOPG/E/2019/0640330 and to a maximum number of country heads through my book 'Global Peace,' presented in November 2017.

This course will generate citizens of 'Outstanding' (honest, sincere, and progressive) and 'Exceptional' (honest, sincere, progressive, and creative/innovative) character. There will be morality, unity, and nationality, irrespective of all differences. Such streamlined nature should be adopted for all citizens of the country and globally to create a disciplined human family worldwide. This would be the path to achieving a developed country and global peace.

Discipline in a student's career leads to discipline throughout life. This brings peace to the family and positively influences society. Students should feel a sense of nationalism and prioritize their country first. They should always stay away from nasty politics. After completing their studies, if they desire to join politics, they will become noble politicians. They can be very good administrators and lead the country to a high profile. The country will be disciplined and progressive if the students maintain discipline. Our leader, Subhash Chandra Bose, said, "Those who are brave always look up." Students are the future of the country. They should be brave and hold their heads high.

3. Third Stage: This period starts from service to retirement, i.e. up to 60 years for all. If one adheres to the following principles, they can be a successful employee, business person and family member. This is the key to success:
    a. One must be truthful.
    b. One should be honest.
    c. One must have a progressive and positive nature.
    d. One must be smart and sober.
    e. One must be target-oriented and do tomorrow's work today and today's work immediately.
    f. Always relieve the burden of higher authority.
    g. Never make mistakes.

h. Never ask your boss what to do. Instead, think about the matter and propose several solutions, helping the higher authority to decide easily. This develops more thinking power.

i. Write your program one day earlier in a diary, tick off what is covered the next day, and carry unattended items to the next day. This method allows one to achieve many targets in life, both for family and professionally, and ensures success.

j. Complete projects within the targeted time. Solve bottlenecks early so that the project can be completed on schedule.

k. Always think of yourself as a judge. Never decide after hearing only one side. This ensures the right decision. If you remain just, even if problems arise, you will not fail and will be supported by the Almighty.

4. Fourth Stage: This is from retirement to the last stage. During this time, one can be involved in any type of work, such as politics, spending time with family, practicing religion, or doing any business. Family members should not burden them. They should give good advice to juniors but avoid doing any work harmful to others or the nation.

By obeying these principles, one can accomplish a lot in their lifetime and always think that time is short.

Dr. Nanda Nandan Das, Original Thinker

Former Secretary, Works Govt. of Odisha

\Chairman, People's Welfare Suggestion Forum

Former Chairman, Odisha Durneeti Sangharsa Mancha

Dt. 11.01.2025

CHAPTER XIX
TRIP TO CHINA

On May 8, 2014, I left Bhubaneswar for Delhi by Rajdhani Express, arrived on May 9 at 10:30 am. My son, Sri Devnandan Das, received me at the station and took me to his residence in Gurgaon. My friend, Sri Sachida Nanda Mishra, and his wife, Smt Kanaka Prava Nanda, joined us on this trip to China and Japan, which was organized by SOTC. During the day, I spent time with my grandchildren in Gurgaon. My flight to Beijing via China Eastern Airlines was scheduled for 2:50 AM (IST) on May 10, with a layover in Shanghai.

Sri Devnandan Das and his family accompanied me to Indira Gandhi International Airport at 10:30 PM to see me off. Flight MU 564 (Airbus A332) departed on time and reached Shanghai Pudong Airport at 10:55 AM (CST) after covering 2,656 miles in 5 hours 35 minutes. We then boarded a domestic flight MU 564 (Airbus A321), which left at 12:20 PM and arrived in Beijing at 2:45 PM, covering 676 miles in 2 hours 25 minutes. Our group checked into Days Inn Joiest Hotel in Beijing, with dinner at an Indian restaurant. Our tour manager was Mr. Emran Khanda and our Beijing guide was Mrs. Cindy.

About China: China stretches approximately 8,000 km from east to west and 5,500 km from north to south. Prices of common items: potatoes cost 0.25 to 2 dollars, apples 1 to 2.5 dollars, and rice about 3 Yuan (around 0.5 dollars). The current President is Xi Jinping.

Exploring Beijing: On May 11, 2014, a rainy day, I purchased an umbrella from the hotel. We had a guided city tour, starting with the Parliament House. Despite the heavy rain and cold weather, the area was beautifully decorated with plants.

PARLIAMENT HOUSE, BEIJING, CHINA

Forbidden City: We visited the Forbidden City, Beijing. This city is having 9999 ½ rooms. The belief of Chinese is that since God can have 10000 rooms, the city is having ½ rooms less. This city is forbidden for 300 years and turn to museum for public. The city was earlier ruled by 24 Empires in 600 years. The buildings of entire city were curved roof maintaining old heritage. These buildings were offices of the emperors, covering 250 acres, featuring curved roof buildings complex of places, pavilions and gardens.

FORBIDDEN CITY, BEIJING, CHINA

After lunch at an Indian restaurant, we visited the Temple of Heaven, where Ming and Qing emperors worshipped. Retired government employees were seen playing cards in the campus. The retirement age is 50 years for males 45 years for females.

TEMPLE OF HEAVEN

TOP PORTION OF TEMPLE OF HEAVEN

Then we visited Government Pearl centre. The artificial pearls are manufactured here. The preparation of artificial pearls was demonstrated here. Generally, the natural pearls are procured one from each cell. But the artificial pearls can be manufactured in malty numbers. Such example is cited in the picture.

DEMONSTRATION OF MANUFACTURE OF ARTIFICIAL PEARLS

Then took dinner in Indian restaurant and back to hotel. Then we had local marketing, I purchased of walking stick, which is especially available in Chin. This stick can be pulled longer and pushed shorter, with provision of magnetic compass to direct poles, torch arrangement for light at night, pointed system on hand grip to protect against any attack.

THE GREAT WALL OF CHINA: *The Greatest Wonder of the World*

12.05.2014-On 12th morning after breakfast we moved for visiting THE GREAT WALL OF CHINA. The length of the country of China from West to East is about 8000 km and North to South is about 5500 km from ancient time. Since the Mongolians were attacking China repeatedly, therefore the Great Wall of China was built to prevent them from attack of Mongolians. During Ming Dynasty (1368-1644), it was enlarged to 6400km (4000miles). The renovation work took for 200 years with watch tower cannon added. This is the symbol of ancient civilization of China. This Great Wall of China passes over ridges of mountains, valleys and plateaus by that it avoids bridges over streams and rivers. The 'great wall' of China is a series of fortification made of stone, brick, tamped earth, wood and other material. Therefore, the different fortification length of Great Wall of China is 13171 miles i.e. 21196 km.

Width of Great wall of China- 4.5m to 9m (15ft to 30ft) and Height-7.5m(25ft). The construction of this wall was started about 2206 years back and the work was continued up to 400 years. The king QINSHIHUANGDI was the first emperor of china during the Qin (Ch'in) dynasty (221 BC to 206 BC) to initiate the construction of the wall. This wall passes through 17 provinces. This wall visible from the Earth orbit on space as per statement of astronauts-Armstrong, Jim Covet, Jim Irwin.

Reaching in front of the Great Wall of China, we the group of Indians of about 45 numbers took a group photo. Then I with my friend Er Sachida Nanda Mishra and his wife Smt. Kanak Prava Nanda went for climbing the wall through the entry gate. I covered and climbed up to 4th watching tower, none of other Indians of our group could reach there.

GROUP PHOTO OF INDIAN GROUP NEAR GREAT WALL OF CHINA

ENTRY GATE TO GREAT WALL OF CHINA

GREAT WALL
OF CHINA

GREAT
WALL OF
CHINA

ENTRY
BUILDING TO
TERRACOTTA
WARRIOR

TERRACOTTA
WARRIOR

DR. NANDA
NANDAN DAS
WITH
WARRIOR
COVER

TV TOWER, CHINA

OLYMPIC PARK
2008, CHINA

MAGNET
TRAIN,
SANGHAI,
CHINA –
SPEED OF
TRAIN 430
KM / HOUR

MAGNET
TRAIN
LINE

CHAPTER XX

SOME MEASURES FOR DEVELOPMENT OF DELHI

Your Grievance is registered successfully.
Registration Number: PMOPG/E/2025/0018684

Dt. 09.02.2025
SOME MEASURES FOR DEVELOPMENT OF DELHI

Respected Shri Narendra Modi Ji, Hon'ble Prime Minister,
On this joyous day of 08.02.2025, the BJP Party celebrates a remarkable victory in the Delhi election. In your speech, you referred to Delhi as "mini-India" and expressed your commitment to its development under the BJP administration.

I have previously shared my suggestions for the development of Delhi with you, and I would like to highlight some key issues along with innovative methods of administration to be implemented within a targeted time period:

1. Posting of Authorities of Exceptional Nature: For matters of government related to specific departments, the minister, supported by government authorities, plays a crucial role. Hence, the posting of high officials should be of exceptional nature, i.e., honest, sincere, progressive, and innovative. Others should be outstanding, i.e., honest, sincere, and progressive. With such visionary action, development will certainly be successful.

   A notable example is the control of the Overdraft of Odisha, which prevented government staff from receiving their salaries regularly. My proposal to the then finance minister in 2005 helped-controlled liabilities and expedite work progress, with

Dr. Sidharth Kanungo, a doctorate in State Budget, playing a significant role. Consequently, the overdraft was controlled in 2006, and staff have been receiving their salaries regularly. This matter was communicated to you under registration number PMOPG/E/2019/0628895 and forwarded to the Gujarat Government for guidance.

2. Cleaning of Yamuna River: Key points for cleaning the Yamuna River near Delhi are as follows, based on 'Nanda's Six Formulae':

   a) Vision - Adopt principles to clean the river within a targeted time.

   b) Target - Identify problems/bottlenecks causing pollution and determine solutions for project completion within the targeted time.

   c) Problems - Detail the exact causes of pollution, including domestic sewage, industrial sewage, and municipal garbage.

   d) Solutions - Derive suitable solutions for each problem, considering all aspects.

   e) Programming to Meet the Target - Establish a shorter time span for project completion, including procuring and repaying loans.

   f) Mode of Achieving Vision - Ensure solutions to all problems and proceed with the project to completion within the targeted time.

3. Control of Flood Due to Storm Water in Delhi: Please refer to registration number PMOPG/E/2024/0106725, dated 03.07.2024.

4. Control of Flood Due to Yamuna River Overflow in Delhi:

Please refer to registration number PMOPG/E/2023/0138801, dated 13.07.2023.

5. Shifting of Capital of India/Method to Make Pollution-Free Delhi:

SOME MEASURES FOR DEVLOPMENT OF DELHI

Please refer to registration number PMOPG/E/2019/0654812, dated 12.11.2019.

Numerous proposals for the betterment, flood control, pollution control, and welfare of Delhi have been suggested earlier. With the new BJP government taking over the Delhi administration, these proposals can be forwarded to them. The details as per the registration numbers may be transmitted to the concerned departments. They should be instructed to scrutinize these innovative suggestions through research-minded individuals to ensure accurate analysis and timely action. With heartiest regards,

Yours sincerely,
Dr. Nanda Nandan Das, Original Thinker
E.I.C cum Secretary, Works, Odisha
Chairman, People's Welfare Suggestion Forum
Dt. 09.02.2025 12:30 am

CHAPTER XXI

SOME GUIDELINES FOR UTKARSA ODISHA

Your Grievance is registered successfully.
Registration Number: PMOPG/E/2025/0013255

Dt. 28.01.2025

Respected Shri Narendra Modi Ji, Hon'ble Prime Minister of India,

Today, on 28th January 2025, you inaugurated the Utkarsh Odisha session in Odisha. During this session, you emphasized the growth of industrial institutions, considering the state's abundant resources such as mining & minerals, water resources, coastal length, marine products, tourism, agriculture, electricity, industries, and IT development etc.

Previously, I have suggested means for the development of Odisha and Bharat. In addition to these suggestions, I propose the following principles to initiate and expedite the progress of projects:

1. Government officials should maintain 'Exceptional'- honesty, sincerity, progressiveness, and innovation character traits,
2. The S.E.Z principles should be strictly followed, with additional guidelines ensuring a minimum 51% ownership by India and 49% by other countries. Strong internal security measures must be implemented to safeguard the country's interests.
3. A scheduled, time-bound period for land acquisition, forest clearance, and other transactions should be established to avoid delays. Accountability must be enforced in case of any defaults.
4. Transparency should be maintained by government authorities and all parties involved in project-related transactions.

GUIDELINES FOR UTKARSA ODISHA

5. In case of loans from financiers, various concerned government departments should be responsible for repaying the loans as per the terms of the agreements, to avoid liabilities.
6. All project employees should be trained to be honest, sincere, and progressive.
7. To foster exceptional and outstanding citizens, moral science should be a compulsory subject in the educational curriculum, as suggested in my registration number PMOPG/E/2019/0640330. These citizens would prioritize national interests.
8. Laws should be strictly enforced to address criminality, corruption, and defaults.

I kindly request that the above suggestions be communicated to the Hon'ble Chief Minister of Odisha for their information and consideration, as I do not have the scope to directly suggest these to the Odisha government, which I have been given encouraged this scope from your kind self. Given that these guidelines are applicable to all states, I recommend forwarding these suggestions as guidelines for other states as well. With heartiest regards,

Yours sincerely,

Dr. Nanda Nandan Das, Original Thinker

Former Secretary, Works Government of Odisha

Chairman, People's Welfare Suggestion Forum

Phone: 9437617604

Dt. 28.01.2025

CHAPTER XXII

THE CULTURE/ SYSTEM: THE SOURCE OF DEVELOPMENT OF THE COUNTRY AND ACHIEVING PEACE GLOBALLY

Dt. 21.12.2024   3:30 AM

All humans belong to one global family, sharing the same planet. For thousands of years, humanity evolved from its primal state due to the superior capacity of human intelligence. This evolution led to the formation of civilizations, beginning in Mesopotamia and spreading worldwide. However, artificial divisions based on religion, race, borders, and personal agendas arose, often leading to conflict. Warfare, border tensions, and terrorism stem from narrow-minded thinking and can be mitigated through global awareness and mutual respect.

Despite abundant resources, India is still not a developed country after seven decades of independence. At the time of independence, India and Pakistan were partitioned based on religious demographics. Pakistan became an Islamic republic in 1956, while India was declared a secular state through the 42nd Amendment of the Constitution in 1976.

RELIGIOUS INTOLERANCE AND ITS CONSEQUENCES

In countries like Bangladesh, Pakistan, and Afghanistan, minorities face persecution. Women and different sects within the same community also suffer atrocities in many Muslim-majority nations, resulting in poverty, crime, and terrorism. These issues stem from extremist mindsets and flawed governance. Wealthy elites often manipulate the poor, exploiting them through biased teachings that lead to violence and unrest.

However, not all members of the Muslim community are complicit in such actions. Many Muslim-majority nations, such as the UAE, are progressive and broad-minded. Islamic principles, as stated by scholars like Acharya Pramod Krishnam, do not condone harm to others. Yet in India, some wealthy individuals within the Muslim community have been accused of keeping the masses illiterate and using them as vote banks, perpetuating socio-economic inequalities.

PROGRESS UNDER BJP GOVERNANCE

The BJP government has significantly improved the lives of underprivileged communities, including housing, water supply, electricity, gas, toilets, free rations, and medical facilities—amenities neglected for decades under previous administrations. Despite these advancements, many within the Muslim community have not supported the BJP due to political biases. Awareness campaigns are needed to dispel misinformation and promote literacy, modern education, and national unity.

PROMOTING PEACE AND COEXISTENCE

Human life is finite, and material possessions are transient. Problems arise from egotism, expansionist ambitions, and a mindset of cruelty. Bharat (India), the birthplace of Sanatan culture, has historically been a target of invasions and religious conflicts. Invaders destroyed many Hindu religious sites and erected their structures in their place. Efforts are now underway to restore these cultural heritage sites.

Hinduism, through Sanatan culture, embodies the principles of universal well-being ("Sarve Bhavantu Sukhinah") and the concept of the world as one family ("Vasudhaiva Kutumbakam"). These ideals promote respect for all religions and peace for humanity. The current government's inclusive policies reflect these values, benefiting all citizens irrespective of religion.

India is undoubtedly better off than these countries in all respects, despite gaining independence at the same time as Pakistan. This progress can be attributed to India's adherence to principles rooted in Hindu culture. The living style for all communities are definitely better. So, all Bharatiya irrespective of religions are desirable accept the present principle of administration, which are better for them and country on the whole.

THE NEED FOR A HINDU NATION

Bharat is the only homeland for Hindus, yet it remains secular to accommodate all communities peacefully. It is time to consider declaring India a Hindu nation, ensuring laws benefit all citizens while fostering unity and morality. Such a step would set a global example of peaceful coexistence.

A GLOBAL FRAMEWORK FOR PEACE

To achieve lasting global peace, we propose the following principles, aligned with the United Nations' mandate (October 24, 1945) and updated to reflect modern scientific advancements:

1. Humanity is one global family.
2. Life is finite; collaboration for peace benefits all.
3. Religion is a personal and social bond, with freedom to practice while respecting others.
4. National leaders must prioritize citizen welfare within the United Nations framework.
5. The United Nations should oversee global defense to prevent conflicts.
6. Nuclear energy should be used exclusively for space exploration, disaster management, and human welfare.
7. International decisions should be based on majority consensus.
8. Educational systems should include value-based curricula emphasizing shared human identity.
9. All forms of terrorism must be universally condemned and penalized.
10. Acknowledge the following universal principles (copyright: Dr. N.N. Das):
    - **Gods:** The Sun, Earth, and our parents sustain life.
    - **Religion:** Humanity is the highest religion.
    - **Caste:** Gender is the only distinction by birth; all have equal rights.

These principles aim to unify humanity and create peace globally.

CONCLUSION

India's Sanatan culture has the potential to inspire global peace. Spreading its values internationally can establish harmony worldwide. We urge a comprehensive review of these suggestions for implementation to build a harmonious and united world.

Dr. Nanda Nandan Das, Original Thinker

Chairman, People's Welfare Suggestion Forum

Supporters: Rtn Ambika Ballav Swain, Prasanta Sahu, Rtn Pranab Kumar Sahu, Prof. Purnima Mitra, Akhay Kumar Panda, Er Shree Nandan Das, Rtn Pramod Kumar Jena, Kumkum Das,